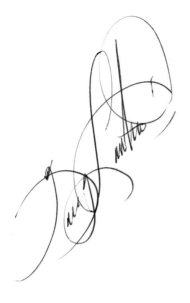

MW01488468

WORDS OF COMFORT
at Evening Time

DR. WRIGHT L. LASSITER JR.

St. John Missionary Baptist Church
March 1995 – September 1998
Dallas, Texas

Order this book online at www.trafford.com
or email orders@trafford.com

Most Trafford titles are also available at major online book retailers.

Printed in the United States of America.

ISBN: 978-1-4269-7645-2 (sc)
ISBN: 978-1-4269-7646-9 (hc)
ISBN: 978-1-4269-7647-6 (e)

Library of Congress Control Number: 2011912572

Trafford rev. 09/13/2011

 www.trafford.com

North America & international
toll-free: 1 888 232 4444 (USA & Canada)
phone: 250 383 6864 ♦ fax: 812 355 4082

Contents

PART TWO
Other Messages

PART THREE
End Notes

PREFACE

This is the updated version of the original edition of Words of Comfort at Evening Time that was printed in 1997. The original edition contained selected messages of comfort that were delivered during my tenure as the Interim Pastor of the St. John Missionary Baptist Church of Dallas.

The second edition contains additional words of comfort delivered at the St. John Church for members of the congregation following my period of service at the church. Also included in this edition are Resolutions of Comfort extended to family members during my tenure as Interim Pastor. An additional inclusion are selected other funeral messages delivered at the St. John Church following the conclusion of my service there, and special funeral messages for colleagues.

The second edition of this publication is the result of family members at the St. John Church who asked that I place the messages in book-form so that it could serve as a source of continuing comfort for them.

The reader will note the conversational and comforting style that I tried to consistently employ. While a funeral, or memorial service, will cause the bereaving family members to be saddened, it is also a time to celebrate the life lived by the departed loved one. Thus the reader will note a theme of celebration in each of the funeral messages. A special item included are the remarks that I delivered at the celebration of life service for my beloved father.

While this collection of funeral messages is only a sampling of some delivered by the author during his ministerial life, there are certain passages of Scripture that have been strong influences in my message preparation. These citations may be instructive:

John 14:1-3, 27	*I Corinthians 15:51-58*	*II Timothy 4:6-8*
Romans 8:37-39	*I Thessalonians 4:13-18*	*Revelation 7:9-17*
Matthew 11:28	*II Corinthians 5:1*	*Revelation 14:13*
Psalm 23	*Proverbs 31:10-31*	*Revelation 21:1-4*
II Samuel 12:15-23		

It is my prayerful hope that these messages and resolutions of comfort will help and bring comfort to those in sorrow, give glory to God, and continue winning souls to the Savior.

Dr. Wright L. Lassiter, Jr.
Former Interim Pastor – St. John Missionary Baptist Church (Dallas)
Current Associate Pastor – Concord Missionary Baptist Church (Dallas)
January 2010

ACKNOWLEDGMENTS

As stated in the first edition, grateful appreciation is extended to my wife, Bessie, for her constant urging to assemble my words in published form so that others could benefit from what gifts the Lord has blessed me with. Thanks also to my daughter and son, for the patience and understanding that they showed when my duties as pastor limited the time available to be with them. Thanks to the entire family unit when I had to spend time visiting members and also to study the Word and frame these words of comfort.

The support and encouragement of my late parents, Rev. Dr. Wright L. Lassiter, Sr., and Ethel Franklin Lassiter is gratefully acknowledged. Their quiet support and encouragement was most beneficial.

I warmly acknowledge the undying support and assistance of Rev. John C. Dvorak. John was my long-time assistant who began working with me while I was President of Bishop College, and he followed me when I served as President of El Centro College. He displayed his marvelous talents in formatting and displaying the written word in the first edition. I must again acknowledge him for his many contributions.

For this second edition, I was ably assisted by Theresa Rose, a friend and member of my staff. The final touches on this work were provided by Toni Barajas, my executive assistant. Both of these colleagues and friends spent hours of their personal time assisting me. I am very grateful for the artistry that you will note in this second edition that resulted from their expertise in the fine details of publishing.

A DEVOTED SON'S REMEMBRANCE OF A GODLY MAN ~ HIS FATHER

When I think of the life of my beloved father, I remember so many things. First and foremost, however, is the fact that he was a GODLY MAN. When I think of him, I am caused to reflect on these words contained in Psalms 1:1-6:

- *"Blessed is the man who walketh not in the counsel in the ungodly, nor standeth in the way of sinners, nor sitteth in the seat of the scornful. But his delight is in the law of the Lord; and in his law doth he meditate day and night."*

- *"And he shall be like a tree planted by the rivers of water, that bringeth forth his fruit in his season; his leaf shall not wither; and whatsoever he doeth shall prosper."*

- *"The ungodly are not so; but are like the chaff which the wind driveth away. Therefore the ungodly shall not stand in the judgment, nor sinners in the congregation of the righteous."*

- *"For the Lord knoweth the way of the righteous; but the way of the ungodly shall perish."*

If one ever wanted to see the epitome of a godly man – it was there in the person of my father. As a reflection of his godliness, I can lift up all of these good qualities that I must admit I have tried to emulate in my life. I have tried to model them because my father was the wind beneath my wings. He was my source of strength and encouragement always.

He was the perfect example of a father who taught his children to "cover the ground that they stood on." To "be all that we could be." "To keep God uppermost in our lives." To do our best to be "modern day Good Samaritans."

Now it is evening time. The end has come for life on this side, but it is just the beginning for life "on the other side." When I think of my father, I think of the seasons of life that another author has described in this manner:

<u>Life is Like a Day</u>

The early morning hours of babyhood –
The morning of youth –
The high noon of maturity –
Then evening comes and the day ends.

<u>Life is Measured in Deeds</u>

Not just the passing of time –
Not merely money-making –
Not fame or brilliance.

<u>Happy is the Man Who Goes About Doing Good</u>

As evening comes we recall the activities of the day that has passed;
We see in clearer perspective the great moral principles of life;
The things of real worth stand out;
The Christian grace takes on their true meaning.

I began this moment of sharing and reflection by quoting a passage of Scripture. Let me close with these words from Psalm 136:1 – "O give thanks unto the Lord for he is good; for his mercy endureth forever."

Delivered by the author at the Celebration of Life for Dr. Wright L. Lassiter, Sr.
Bowmar Avenue Baptist Church
Vicksburg, Mississippi

PART ONE

The Messages

Celebrating the Life of a True Christian Man ~ Jesse Henry

March 29, 1995

The Bible says many wonderful things about the death of a Christian. But I am not sure that we believe all these things. We think of death as an end to all things good. We think of death as a time of separation. We think of it as a hideous monster come to cut off all our joys.

But death for a Christian really is a wonderful thing. When death comes (and it will come to each of us), we are really being rescued by a good friend. We live in a cruel world, a world of few joys, but a world of many hardships, injustices, trials, tears, sorrows and separations. Now when death comes to take us into the presence of the Lord, where we shall have perfect health and perfect rest, wouldn't you say that death is, after all, a good friend? We look upon death as an enemy, but really it is one of God's servants who takes us to a better land.

So today we just come together to say good-by to our friend and family member, Jesse Henry. We also come to thank God that he is now with Jesus, where sickness and sorrow can never touch him again. Brother Henry has just gone over Jordan, he has just gone over home.

A WONDERFUL TEXT

In Psalm 116:15, we read these words: "Precious in the sight of the Lord is the death of His saints." When a Christian dies it is a matter of concern to the Lord. He knows about every breath that we draw, every pain that we endure, every groan that we utter. It all means something to Him. Now our text says, not that death is precious in our sight, but in God's sight. In that passage the Psalmist is talking about death from God's standpoint. Today, as we celebrate the home going of Brother Henry, it brings grief to us, but it is precious in God's sight.

A WONDERFUL SLEEP

The Bible says, "He giveth His beloved sleep." Elizabeth Barrett Browning said that to her this was the sweetest text in the Bible.

Now sleep is a very wonderful thing. We can't do without it. Every living thing must have some time for sleep. It "knits up the raveled sleeve of care." It brings us sweet rest and gives us new strength for the new day. Oh yes, physical sleep is a wonderful thing, but it can never compare with the sleep God gives to His beloved.

What a different sleep that is. We go to sleep tonight and when we wake up tomorrow, we have the same old problems and worries and aches and pains that were ours when we went to bed. But when we go to sleep in Jesus, we soon wake up on a new shore and find that it is heaven. We breathe a new air and find that it is celestial air.

We feel the touch of a new hand on ours and find that it is God's hand.

THE MEANING OF DEATH FOR A CHRISTIAN

Let me close this message with a brief discourse on the meaning of death for a Christian.

First, it means a change in environment. Everything down here has been contaminated by sin. On every hand we find dishonesty, drunkenness, lies and lust. We also find many of the by-products of sin, namely sickness, sorrow, pain, poverty and death.

But when God's people die they go to a place where these things can never touch them. They go from sin to sinlessness, from the hovels of earth to heaven's mansions, from earth's discords to heaven's harmonies, from all that is bad to all that is good, from all that hurts to all that brings happiness.

Second, it means a change of nature. Third, it means a reunion with our loved ones. Your beloved family member and friend, Brother Jesse Henry, is not gone forever. You shall see him again in a land of light and love. This will be a special reunion for our loved ones and our friends and our Savior will be there to greet us and welcome us to the Heavenly City.

Fourth, and finally, it means that we shall see Jesus. If it were not for Jesus there would be no heaven. The golden streets and the pearly gates and the mansions and the robes and the crowns would mean absolutely nothing if Jesus were not there. But, beloved Henry family, we can thank God, for we shall see Him and we shall know Him and we shall want to fall at His feet and thank Him for saving us and bringing us safely home.

So, now as we say "good-by" to this beloved friend and family member, we realize how wonderful it is up there for him. May his memory linger on in our hearts to bless us and bring us closer to God.

We live in a great and growing city. But the city which is growing faster than all others is the Holy City of the New Jerusalem, which we call heaven. May God grant that we might so live and so trust Christ that someday we, too, shall join Brother Henry in that wonderful city.

We recite words from an expression titled "Good Night" for your comfort and reflection as we end this message of celebration.

A Walk Through the Valley ~ Ethel Bell

April 27, 1995

Most of us are aware that the 23rd Psalm is read quite frequently in memorial settings. I would assert that the use of the psalm is no accident, neither is the frequent use due to habit. The psalmist has provided for us a word of hope that goes beyond the limits of life into the shadows which appear for every human being.

Assuming that David is the author of this masterpiece, one must consider the background he brought to his words. David was a mortal creature with joys and frustrations. He was a powerful person physically and politically. He was a king and a servant of God. He was also a man of confidence in himself, but as a man of great faith he had tremendous faith in God.

We can only speculate as to the immediate circumstances of this psalm. Whatever the immediate occasion it was one of those times when the very foundations of life seemed to be threatened. Yet, we must take note that the psalmist spoke with such assurance, an assurance for which most of us hunger.

Focusing on Psalm 23:4, consider his carefully chosen description of death. Not a word was wasted as he pointed us to the only source of confidence in those times. He spoke of death in several ways that can be encouraging for us who are assembled for this moment of memorial and celebration.

He talked of his "walk through the valley of the shadow of death." The fact that he described the place as a valley is significant. Of all the possibilities of places, the psalmist selected the visual image of a valley. He did not describe death in terms of a violent sea, a stormy mountain, nor a lifeless death. He painted the image of a valley, that area at the foot of a peaceful mountain. It is not far from the mountain where we can more easily envision the omnipotent God of peace.

The psalmist continued the sermon in his description of death as a shadow. The image he offered is such a powerful one. While others of his day spoke of the chambers of death or the gates of death, David became a pioneer as he defined the tense power of death by relegating it to only a shadow.

We who come to celebrate the life of Sister Ethel Bell must keep in mind a shadow exists only as long as there is light to cast a shadow. The Lord was not only David's Shepherd who supplied his wants but also the only Source of light. Regardless of its nature, death only temporarily stands in our light. The light is still there. A shadow is evidence of its existence. What a reassuring image of this force we seem to fear!

Yet, one of the most significant words in Psalm 23 is one that we frequently read past without giving much thought to the reassurance which is offered. The psalmist spoke of a walk through the valley. It is not a walk into the valley. It is not a walk in the valley. It is not even a walk around the valley. Instead, the journey is through the valley. This image has to be one of the most powerful in all of scripture.

We can also take comfort the journey is temporary. The writer did not go into detail concerning time. The length of the walk becomes insignificant once the discovery is made that the journey is only temporary. We can persevere al long as we can see light at the end of the tunnel. That light is always there.

Dear family members, as well as members of the St. John family, the walk you are experiencing on this Memorial Day is a temporary one. The valley of the shadow is all about you. But you must keep in mind that this segment is not an endless journey. You, too, will soon walk into the light which has only been momentarily blocked.

The basis for our hope is found in the fact that the Shepherd is walking with us. We are not alone in these circumstances or in any other. The Shepherd has not only walked before us, but preparations have been made for our necessities, even now as we meet here. There is little in life more frightening than loneliness. Keep in mind that our walk is not a solo. There is the best company possible for our journey. A caring Shepherd will comfort us with his rod and staff.

There is little in life that isolates us more than the pain of grief. Yet this psalm is a vivid reminder that His rod and staff are providing for our needs this very moment. A loved one, Sister Ethel Bell, for whom there is genuine grief, will not return on this side of the door. But, in the meantime as you adjust to that absence, the Shepherd will be caring for you and your loved family member every moment.

There is no mystery as to why this great psalm is embraced so frequently in this setting. In this moment there are great needs for green pastures and still waters. The psalmist pointed us to a Shepherd who does more than just tend to us. He laid down His life for us. The path we walk today is not an uncharted way. Preparations began long ago as He seeks even now, this very moment, to restore our souls.

So it is with our loved one, Sister Ethel Bell, in whose memory we gather. Remember, the Good Shepherd has not only carried Ethel Bell into, but through the shadow.

Let us pray:

> *Lord, help us to see death as it really is –*
> *only a shadow.*
> *Most of all, help us to trust the Shepherd*
> *who has experienced and understands*
> *all mysteries –*
> *in whose name we offer our prayer.*
> *Amen*

The Death of a Saintly Woman ~ Catherine Bell

April 29, 1995

There are some statements in Holy Scripture which, if taken out of context, might seem contrary to human thinking. The biblical concept of death might be an example of such. To most of us death is equated with sorrow and tears. This event is understood by society as a time of great anxiety. The fear of death is commonly so great that we anticipate it and all of its emotion long before it actually occurs.

Most of us instinctively avoid even the discussion of death, for within every heart lurks the fear of death and dying. We prefer not to talk about it. We do not like to think about it. Deep within us, death appears to be the ultimate defeat.

God, however, takes a very different view of death. In His Word God says that death can be precious. The particular verse upon which we will focus our attention is taken from a context of thanksgiving. As we read the psalm we can envision one who had come to the temple to offer a vow and a sacrifice. It is obvious that at some point he had suffered affliction and in his hour of need he had taken a vow that if the Lord delivered him he would make a pilgrimage to the temple and offer appropriate sacrifice. We do not know the nature of his affliction, only that it was serious.

In keeping his vows, the psalmist had done more than just offer a temporary sacrifice. There is implied in the psalm the willingness of the psalmist to submit himself totally to God. He prayed and desired deliverance, but he rendered his own will to that of God to the point that death may be seen as within the precious and loving arms of God.

In the submission of his own will to that of God, the psalmist's concept of death took on a quality that was and continues to be inconceivable by the secular world. He is joyful in God's delivering his soul from death but totally at peace with death as well, for all takes place within the sight of the Lord.

Yet, the fact must be acknowledged that only a person of saintly character could offer this kind of vow. Only one who has lived a life close to God, like Sister Catherine Bell, can approach death from this different perspective.

For saints like Sister Bell, death is one of those areas where there is a distinct advantage over those who have never exercised that faith. Through the eyes of our faith, death takes on an unusual quality. God says that death can be precious and more so than just relieving pain.

There are inevitable questions which people will ask concerning the scriptural assertion that death can be a precious thing. To whom is it precious? The text indicates that it is precious to God.

Death is not a precious thing to the physician. To a degree it indicates a defeat because medical science could not change the inevitable. Death is also not too precious to those left behind. The pain of separation is real. Yet to the saints of God, death is but a natural completion of a journey begun long ago.

Death is a way of letting God exercise His wisdom and love. His thoughts are above us, and His ways are beyond us. The saints have learned the secret of happiness by letting God be God, even in regard to the taking of our own lives and the lives of our loved ones.

Yet, death is precious to God only in the lives of certain people. One can assume that not every life represents a successful molding process. Not everyone walks the road with God. Death becomes a terrifying experience for those who have never seen the light of the cross. Not so, with Sister Catherine Bell. She walked with God every step of her earthly sojourn.

Our text suggests that God takes our lives seriously. There is not one single aspect of our lives which is omitted from God's care. Life is a gift, and, therefore, one's death is a valued concern of God. Truly precious in the sight of the Lord is the death of His saints. Why is this true? Because death marks the completion of something God began long ago. Not one life is an accident. He sends every life into the world for the purpose of molding that life until ready for eternal life with God. For the saint, death marks the completion of that process. Death may be seen as God now considering the life ready for even greater things. Death suddenly becomes a time of celebration. God's work in that life has now been completed.

To Robert and Steve, and other family members, the life of your mother was no accident. She was a part of God's plan. God has sent his angel to tap this saintly lady on the shoulder and say that she has done a good job. So, we are here to celebrate a job well done. This is a cause for joy, not sadness.

This is a time for thanksgiving – not for what has been taken, but for what has been given. Consider the gifts that Sister Bell leaves behind as an inheritance.

First, she has left a good name. There is no shame for you here. A good name is a special kind of pride.

Second, she has left behind a good example. She was as human as the rest of us, but let's face it – some just have a better grip on life's realities than other do. There was no question as to the priorities in Sister Catherine's life.

Third, she has left you the assurance of being loved. You, family and friends as well, have an advantage over many people. Many people live a lifetime without experiencing the love you have received from her.

So, the death of Catherine Bell becomes a way of your claiming these gifts, and because of that inheritance you discover that her passing has become a precious thing for you as well.

We come back to the words of the psalmist. He had submitted his entire life to the will of God. Therefore, every phase of life had significance. Most especially was this true concerning death. Death is not the ultimate defeat for the believer. Instead, it is the successful completion of a project begun long ago. Death is not the revoking of life but the gently touch of the Creator who says to Sister Catherine Bell – "Come with me, and let's celebrate a job well done."

The psalmist's statement is really true: "Precious in the sight of the Lord is the death of His saints" (verse 15).

> *Father God, enable us to claim the gifts*
> *left behind by this dear saintly lady.*
> *Most of all help us to envision*
> *our own lives as a project with You.*
> *Give us grace to live our days in such a way*
> *that our lives and our deaths may be*
> *precious in Your sight.*
> *Amen*

In Times Like These Christ Goes Before Us ~ Erma Dukes

May 4, 1995

We direct your attention to John 14:2 as our focus passage for this memorial service. I consider the verses contained in John 14:1-7 to be very appropriate and meaningful for this time in the lives of the family of Sister Erma Dukes. So very difficult is the task of saying goodbye to someone special in our lives, but when death invades into our ranks, we are forced to say good-bye.

One psychologist has said that two of the earliest words a child learns are hello and good-bye. We spend most of our days moving back and forth between these two words. As intense as the pain of loss can be under the best of circumstances, our grief would be unbearable if death were a great dark chasm into which our loved ones fell and disappeared.

The comforting words of Jesus form a stark contrast to our worst fears of death. His first six words in the passage set the stage for what He is trying to accomplish: "Let not your heart be troubled." Jesus is calming the minds of His followers made anxious by His comments in John 13:33, "Little children, yet a little while I am with you."

His word of advice and comfort to the disciples is that they should exercise faith – faith in God and faith in Him. "You believe in God, believe also in Me." Our Lord also directs His words to those of us who are gathered in this memorial setting for Sister Erma Dukes. He is saying to the family – "Let not your hear be troubled." We need to hear those words today just as much as those anxious disciples long ago. As Jesus observed His disciples, He saw them growing tired and weary. He is just as aware of your present circumstances family members.

It has been rough on members of the family. Just as surely as he did to those disciples He says to you, "Let not your heart be troubled." These are not empty words. They are a promise to each of us.

Those early disciples had plenty to trouble them. Jesus was constantly talking about His mysterious departure. He was going away. But where? In their hearts they must have known that death was involved somewhere along the way. Given the circumstances within and without, there was so much to cause great concern.

Yet Christ told them – faced by all of these facts – not to worry. Fortunately for their sakes and ours, He explained to them why they had no cause for great alarm. We need to hear His word of hope just now.

First, we need not be troubled. That is a rallying cry needed in this anxious world. Fear can dictate our lives. We are always afraid that the worst will come. But Christ would say that, even if the worst does come, you have no reason to fear. He verified His personal beliefs with His own life. Because He really did believe in God and did believe that God means what He says, Jesus was able to face the worst that life could offer.

Why should we not be troubled? Jesus said, "Believe in God." This belief means never having to manage on our own. We can always go to Him and are helped by Him.

Second, death most certainly should not be our ultimate fear. Death is not falling into some dark pit. Death for the believer translates into heaven. While we know very few details, the New Testament leaves no question but that heaven is a glorious place.

Jesus knows your anxiety at this time. Whenever we are to take a trip, there is always some concern over preparations. When I arrive, will I have been expected? Will accommodations be in order? Jesus said with absolute assurance that preparations have been made for Sister Dukes. She has her own personal and exclusive place in the Father's future plans for her.

Consider once again the image that the text offers. When a special guest is coming to visit, we will make certain that everything is in order. We will know of those things which are special to our guest. The right books, food and flowers will appropriately be placed. We always prepare well for our guests.

God and His Son have also made good preparations. Our coming and home going in life are no accident; therefore, God has planned well for His family.

Remember also that these preparations have not been left to chance. Christ has taken it upon Himself to make the arrangements. Sister Dukes is important enough that the Son of God Himself has taken care of our ultimate needs. When we encounter death, we do not embark alone. Death does not take us by the hand. Instead, Jesus takes our hand and leads us through a path He has already traveled.

Once again, we would benefit ourselves by claiming our trust in God. If we can trust Him in this life, we can trust Him in the life to come. There is no need for fear now or later on. Why? Because Christ has gone before us and made all the necessary arrangements. This claim is not the result of vague, wishful thinking. God's Word has established this promise for all people in all ages to come. Indeed, Christ goes before us.

And so, calmly and quietly, we note the home going of Sister Erma Dukes, who is known and loved. With courage and determination we move away from this hour to accept the responsibilities of those unlived days before us with full assurance that our loved one has only claimed the place prepared by the Lord of life for her.

Let us pray:

Our Father, we thank You that death is not the swallowing up of ourselves or our loved ones. We offer praise and gratitude for the preparations made for each one of us. Help us today to exercise our trust in You now and in the life to come.
Amen

The Death of a Saintly Woman ~ Revisited ~ Lena Lou Estell

July 13, 1995

There are some statements in Holy Scripture which, if taken out of context, might seem contrary to human thinking. Their biblical concept of death might be an example of such. To most of us death is equated with sorrow and tears. This event is understood by society as a time of great anxiety. The fear of death is commonly so great that we anticipate it and all of its emotion long before it actually occurs.

Most of us instinctively avoid even the discussion of death, for within every heart lurks the fear of death and dying. We prefer not to talk about it. We do not like to think about it. Deep within us, death appears to be the ultimate defeat.

God, However, takes a decidedly different view of death. In His Word God says that death can be precious. The particular verse upon which we have focused our attention on these home going services is taken from a context of thanksgiving. As we read the psalm we can envision one who had come to the temple to offer a vow and a sacrifice. It is obvious that at some point he had suffered affliction and in his hour of need he had taken a vow that if the Lord delivered him he would make a pilgrimage to the temple and offer appropriate sacrifices. We do not know the nature of his affliction, only that it was serious.

In keeping his vows, the psalmist had done more that just offer a temporary sacrifice. There is implied in the psalm the willingness of the psalmist to submit himself totally to God. He prayed and desired deliverance, but he rendered his own will to that of God to the point that death may be seen as within the precious and loving arms of God.

In the submission of his own will to that of God, the psalmist's concept of death took on a quality that was and continues to be inconceivable by the secular world. He is joyful in God's delivering his soul from death but totally a peace with death as well, for all takes place within the sight of the Lord.

Yet the fact must be acknowledged that only a person of saintly character could offer this kind of vow. Only one who has lived a life close to God can approach death from this different perspective.

For the saints of God, death is one of those areas where there is a distinct advantage over those who have never exercised that faith. Through the eyes of our faith, death takes on an unusual quality. God says that death can be precious and more so that just relieving pain.

Death is precious to God. Death is a way of allowing God to exercise His wisdom and love. His thought is above us, and His ways are beyond us. The saints have learned the secret of happiness by letting God be God, even in regard to the taking of our own lives and the lives of our loved ones seriously. There is not one single aspect of our lives which is omitted from God's care. Life is a gift, and, therefore, one's death is a valued concern of God. Truly precious in the sight of the Lord is the death of His saints. Why is this true?

Because death marks the completion of something God began long ago. Not one life is an accident. He sends every life into the world for this purpose of molding that life until ready for eternal life with God. For the saint, death marks the completion of that process. Death may be seen as God now considering the life ready for even greater things. Death suddenly becomes a time of celebration. God's work in that life has been completed.

Does this scripture not provide a backdrop for our gathering here today? The life of Sister Lend Lou Estell was no accident. She was a part of God's plan. The beauty of her experience may be found in the fact that successful molding has taken place. God has sent His angel to tap this good lady on the shoulder and say that she has done a good job. Essentially, we are here to celebrate a job well done. That is a cause for joy, not sadness.

This is a time for thanksgiving – not for what has been taken but for what has been given. Consider the gifts that are left behind as an inheritance.

Lena Lou has left a good name. There is no shame for you here. We have sometimes made pride seem shameful. Yet there is a kind of pride that is special: a good name.

Lena Lou, secondly, has left behind a good example. She was as human as the rest of us, but let's face it – some just have a better grip on life's realities than others do. There was no question as to the priorities in her life.

Third, she has left you the assurance of being loved. You, family and friends as well, have an advantage over many people. Many people live a lifetime without experiencing the love you have received from Lena Lou.

Her death becomes a way of your claiming these gifts and because of that inheritance you discover that her passing has become a precious thing for you as well.

We come back to the words of the psalmist. He had submitted his entire life to the will of God. Therefore, every phase of his life had significance. Most especially was this true concerning death. Death is not the ultimate defeat for the believer. Instead, it is the successful completion of a project begun long ago. Death is not the revoking to life but the gentle touch of the Creator who says, "Come with me, and let's celebrate a job well done."

The statement of the psalmist really is true: "Precious in the sight of the Lord is the death of His saints."

Sleep on Lena Lou Estell – we hope to join you in the sweet bye and bye!

Lessons for the Living ~ Lewis Hester

July 13, 1995

We are always to remember that our funeral services are not for the dead, but for the living. There is no word that we can say which can reach the ear of our departed friend, Brother Lewis Hester. And, although we would pay a tribute to him and his faithful Christian life, this service is primarily for those who are gathered here today out of love and respect for a good man.

The great question that comes to mind when one dies is – "Was he ready to go?" We thank God that Brother Hester settled this matter many years ago when he repented of his sins and trusted Jesus Christ as his personal Savior. And since that time he has served Christ well, always being true and faithful to the Lord, to His Church and the highest and best things of life.

THE BIBLE SAYS WONDERFUL THINGS ABOUT THE DEATH OF A CHRISTIAN

We read these words, "Blessed are the dead who die in the Lord, for they rest from their labors and their works do follow them." The word "blessed" here means "happy". Not all those who die are going to be happy, but those who die "in the Lord" will come to know the supreme happiness that only God can give.

Then we read, "Precious in the sight of the Lord is the death of His saints." Again we read, "He giveth His beloved sleep". Elizabeth Barrett Browning said that to her this was the sweetest verse in the Bible. We struggle and strain, we worry and fret through this life. We become tired and worn out. And then God puts us to sleep for a while and we wake up in glory. Again we read, "Absent from the body, present with the Lord." The body is put away in the grave, but the real person, the spirit, the soul is not there. The Christian has simply left his worn-out body down here and has gone out to be with the Lord. Isn't that wonderful? "Absent from the body, present with the Lord."

WHAT DOES A CHRISTINA GAIN BY DYING?

Paul said, "For me to live is Christ and to die is gain". Does a man gain anything when he dies? Doesn't he have to leave everything behind, his home, his loved ones, his friends? Yes, that is true, but if he can say that he has lived for Christ, as Paul said, and as Brother Hester did, he can know that he will gain infinitely more in death than he can ever gain in this life.

✝ *Brother Hester has gained freedom, freedom from all the aches and pains and sorrows and sufferings and problems and troubles of this world. Yes – we gain freedom when we die in Christ.*

✝ *Brother Hester, a true Christian, in dying gains the sweetest fellowship ever enjoyed by anyone. Fellowship with all the great men and women of the Bible. Fellowship with all the great people of the ages. Fellowship with all the loved ones whom we "have loved since and lost awhile". And best of all, fellowship with the Lord Jesus Christ, who made heaven possible for us.*

✝ *Brother Hester has now gained the fullness of knowledge. There are so many things down here which we don't understand. We wonder why sin comes in to break our hearts and blast our hopes. We wonder why so often some fine and useful person is taken away and another is left who makes no contribution the world's benefit. We will never understand these things down here, but someday in the golden glow of that better land we'll sit down beside the Lord Jesus and He will explain it all. Then we will see that some of the things which caused us so much sorrow down here were simply blessings in disguise, and God allowed them to come to us for our good and His glory.*

LESSONS FOR THE LIVING

To the family there are two clear lessons for the living. First of all, death is certain. If the Lord tarries, if He doesn't return in our lifetime, we shall all die. "It is appointer unto man once to die, and after that the judgment." Death may come soon to some of us, it will not surely be long for any of us. It may come suddenly or it may come after a lingering illness. It comes to the king's palace. It comes to the poor man's cottage. But it is coming and we must get ready for it.

But there is only one way to prepare for death and the judgment. That is through faith in the Lord Jesus Christ. There is no other way of salvation. "He that believeth on the Son hath everlasting life; and he that believeth not the Son shall not see life, but the wrath of God abideth on him."

COMFORT FOR THE LIVING

Sister Hester and family members, you are comforted in remembering that you did your best for Brother Hester. Now you can just say with one of old, "The Lord gave and the Lord hath taken away; blessed be the name of the Lord".

You are comforted in remembering that death isn't all. Beyond this vale of tears there is another life and another land. The grave is not our goal. We look forward to a new home of joy and bliss which will be ours when we leave this earthly home.

You are comforted in remembering that you will see your beloved, Lewis Hester, again. The Bible implies that we shall see and know our loved ones in heaven. Heaven is a complete place, but would it be entirely complete if we never saw our loved ones up there? Surely, surely, we shall see Brother Hester again in a land where we shall know even as we are known.

But our greatest comfort comes from Christ. One day Jesus spoke to a group of people just like us and He said, "Come unto Me, all ye that labor and are heavy laden and I will give you rest." He stands today with open arms and says the same thing to you. Just come to Him, lean your head upon His bosom and He will give you rest and the comfort and the grace and the courage you need for this hour.

I must ask you to turn all of your cares and burdens over to the Lord. God will give you peace and bring you through safely. So I bid you today to turn all your sorrow over to Jesus. He will bring you safely through, giving you grace and comfort for today and courage for all of your tomorrows.

So, Sister Hester, and members of the family, may God bless the memory of this good man. And may He bless and comfort all of you who mourn today. And may all of us place our hands in the nail-pierced hand of Jesus and follow Him until He takes us home.

The Shining Light of the Just ~ Ernestine G. Mays

July 28, 1995

I draw your attention to these passages of scripture from the Holy Bible on this occasion of celebrating the home going of Sister Ernestine Grayson Mays: "She was full of good works and acts of charity" (Acts 9:36b). "The path of the just is a shining light, that shineth more and more unto the perfect day" (Proverbs 4:18).

My friends consider, if you will, why we are gathered here today. We have not come together to move quickly through some hollow ritual. Instead, there are several very important reasons why we are here. Permit me to mention just three for this assemblage of family and friends of Ernestine Grayson Mays.

First, we have come here to remember a fine Christian woman and mother. It is good to remember because our minds are gifts from God. Our memories warm us in moments of loneliness. Our memories help us in moments of decision.

Together we claim the memory of Mother Mays' investment in the lives of the family that she headed for so many years. Memories of loved ones are not taken with the passing of their mortal bodies. Consider the influence of this our sister. Through memory, her influence will continue.

As we walk with people we are shaped by them. The good in one person can easily become the good of another. I am sure that every member of this extensive Mays family can honestly say that some of the good in your life is because of the influence of Ernestine Grayson Mays, whose memory we claim today. Our memory is truly a gift of God, and can be the source of great joy. As I sat with this family on Sunday night past, and the days subsequent to when Mrs. Mays' sleep began, I heard you recall the days in the projects. I heard you talk about how your mother was always doing something for somebody else. I heard you talk about there always being a little something in the pot for the neighborhood children who stopped by the house, in spite of the fact that there were ten of you. I know that you will cherish the fond memories of your mother – that is the way it should be.

There is a second reason why we have come together. We are here to offer comfort and support. The work of grief is never an easy task. Pain is a part of our human experience, especially within the context of personal loss. Jesus understood that part of our humanity. He said: "Blessed are they that mourn; for they shall be comforted" (Matthew 5:4).

Through Christ, our Lord, we offer support to one another in this setting. One of the values of the incarnation is that God knows and understands because He has been here. At this very moment He knows our pain and can help. Without the incarnation there might be doubt in our minds that God really does understand our pain just now. He does understand. Therefore, we come together to offer support to a grieving family and friends. That support is very important. Moving through this kind of experience without the aid of the Christian community must be difficult.

Family members, you will continue to be lifted in our prayers as you adjust to the change in your lives created by the passing of this dear mother.

If our reasons for being here ended with just those two, there would be sadness indeed, and the sorrow would be overwhelming. But there is an even greater reason for gathering here. Most of all, we come together to claim our hope, not some vague fantasy, but hope based upon fact. The resurrection of our Lord adds a dimension to the event of death that will never be erased.

From the human perspective, death is an awesome thing. Death is powerful, mysterious and frightening. If death had the final word, this moment would be a time of nothing but grief. But this is not the end. This dear one around whose mortal body we gather has experienced a change. You see, death is a passage from one life to another. Ernestine Grayson Mays has claimed the promise, a promise made to each one of us.

Christianity is founded on hope. The simple and great truth about Jesus is hope. Our hope is the resurrection of Christ. If Christ is not risen, then our hope is in vain. A long time ago, Sister Mays let the world know that she had grasped the gospel of hope, the gospel of Christ whose creative power is capable of lifting us above any and all things which come at us from so many directions.

So we are here, family and friends, to remember. To remember a fine Christian woman and mother. We come together to individually and collectively offer support in a time of grief and sadness. But most of all, we gather to claim our hope – hope that is found in a loving God who sent His Son that none should perish.

But, I want to leave you with a final thought on this home going celebration event. How grateful we should be for those strong persons who have preceded us, and hopefully have made impressions upon us. Few people have the power of influence upon us as do our mothers. A mother has touched our lives in ways beyond our counting. The influence of a mother at times has been subtle and quiet. There have been other times when the influence has been as bold and obvious as the thunder. The light of this mother has been upon the path of her children, and their children, since the moment of their first breath. Her strong and powerful influence will continue uninterrupted even by this grave. How much we owe those who have cast light upon our path! And how we need that light! Otherwise, darkness can be overwhelming.

Let me close with this story. A hunter tells the story of hunting deer with a friend in unfamiliar woods. The path was clear in the light of the sun. The two were to meet before dark at an obvious and specified place in the woods before returning to the truck. The unfamiliar hunter was overwhelmed by the beauty of the woods. The colors were bright, the wind was crisp, and the birds all stand in concert. Hunting became secondary to the beauty of the moment.

The sun began to set, but the hunter was so intrigued by nature that he wanted to wait until the last moment. But dark came so suddenly. In what seemed like seconds, the colors turned to darkness, and all the animals became quiet. The path which had been so clear only minutes before became totally indistinct. After a few turns, the direction of the meeting place was completely lost, and suddenly the darkness became overwhelming. The woods were too thick to determine a path. There was nowhere to go. The hunter was at the mercy of the night.

After a while the sound of whistling could be heard. A beam of light could be seen like a flare. The whistling and the light was coming from his friend, who had guessed what the problem was and had come looking for him His friend had come to offer guidance through a dark path. Thanks to the friend and the light, the path became clear and, in minutes, both were in the truck and on the way home.

The hunter's experience has been relived many times in everyone's life. The time of darkness was probably not in the woods, but darkness takes many forms. Throughout our lives, we need someone to come to us and offer light to our path.

Who has offered more light to our journey than our mothers? And a mother's influence has been even more powerful when the light she brought was none other than Christ, our Lord. This mother has offered not only herself, but the Source of all light.

Therefore, our gathering here is a tender hour. Yet, in no way is this an hour of tragedy. It is appropriate that we honor the passing of this one who has lived long and full. We honor Sister Mays who has offered kindness and love and loyalty to Christ in her life.

Let us see this hour as it is meant to be, not a time of darkness, but another time when she brings light. This moment is a time of grief, but let us not dwell on the loss. Instead, let us grasp the measure of our gratitude for this life lived before us.

She has been one of the just, and her pathway has been a shining light. If a light is to help us, we must stand in its light, or we shall continue to stumble. Long ago this dear lady faced that light and set her feet upon the pathway of the just. The light she discovered was not to be possessed but shared. Through her faith she has shared that light and offered direction to the dark paths of others.

Like all journeys, this pilgrimage of hers came to an end. Yet she knew she was in God's keeping, and the end of her path was only a shadow. Such was her faith and comfort, and so is ours to be found. Because of Sister Ernestine Grayson Mays, your heritage is a most valuable one, family members. Yours is the memory of a good mother whom you can always remember, love and respect. Her life has been a light for your path and her death shall conclude that influence. She waits for you, and the pathway to her has been illuminated by her life and love.

The writer of Proverbs was right on target. "The path of the just is as the shining light."

Let us pray:

> *Oh God, we thank You for the light of Your Son*
> *and the way that light has shone through the*
> *love of this Christian woman and mother.*
> *Amen*

The Measure of Success for a
Saintly Woman ~ Bernadine Robinson

August 1, 1995

To the family of "Bernie" I come now to offer words of comfort as you share with the church family, and the many friends of Bernie, this last public moment. Having been privileged to count Mrs. Bernadine among my friends since coming to Dallas twelve years ago, this is a special moment for me. All of us have such fond memories of a remarkable Christian woman. We have wonderful memories of the librarian, the wordsmith, the gracious lady who helped so many young girls get a proper foundation for life, the quintessential servant, the person who always had a kind word and a smile. Our litany of accolades could go on and on, for Bernie was truly a remarkable person.

On one of the last visits that my wife and I made with Bernie in her home, she remarked how God has been so good to her and how she was ready for whatever God had in store for her. If I could paraphrase her expressions, they would be on this order:

God has been good to me. To tell in part demands new words.
His gracious power in so many ways
has blessed me through long years of happy days.
I have not eloquence to voice his praise;

> *I can but say with grateful heart ~*
> *"God has been good to me."*

I want to use those thoughts of God's goodness to Bernie, to leave a few thoughts with the family and friends that may be helpful to all of us, and would represent what Bernie would want us all to think on during our remaining days.

Usually when we hear of the death of someone, we frequently get around to asking about their age? If we hear of a friend's parent passing away, our first question will generally be, "How old was she?" When a friend's work associate dies, sooner or later we get around to asking, "How old was she?"

Perhaps one reason we ask is that it seems to be easier to justify in our minds the death of someone more advanced in years. If one has accumulated enough years we can more easily accept one's death and assume it to be a natural event. Death seems less tragic when we can say they had a "full life". The concern for one's age is obviously a result of the fact that we tend to measure one's life in years as though that were the sole gauge. The success of human life depends largely on how it is measured.

The psalmist states in Psalm 90:10: "the days of our years are three-score years and ten". In doing so, he had only given us a description of life's expectancy. We do not have a guarantee for that many years. We can all name persons who never came close to that age, and we can think of some who have far exceeded that number. The psalmist was only saying that the average life expectancy is seventy years, and, even then, when compared to God, these years are but a sigh in the passage of time.

We are here to remember one who accumulated many years. And yet her life can be measured in many ways, other than the mere passage of time. When one's reviews the accomplishments of Bernadine, she did far more that what God gave her than most. Her life was one worth celebrating for she combined numbers of years and accomplishments.

Keep in mind my friends that life's true accomplishments are not always the ones which appear in the newspaper headlines. Most great acts of love go unnoticed by the masses, as was true with Bernadine. In fact, many labors of love are known only by God.

How unfortunate it is that the normal measure of life values quantity over quality. Consider the life of our Lord. You cannot question the quality of His life, and what He did in a small number of years. Consider in your various personal ways the life of Bernadine. The quality of her life will be remembered long after the quantity.

Another measure exists which must not be forgotten. Our most important measure is at the point of preparation for life to come. In fact, the best way to live this life is in preparation for the life to follow. One lives best who early chooses the only true foundation for life. Bernadine did just that. All other measures become insignificant by comparison.

Preparation for life beyond is a lifelong process. This preparation is not a crash course in eternal survival occurring at the last minute. The preparation begins the moment one opens oneself to salvation through Christ as Lord. Preparation for life beyond continues through all of one's days. When that moment of death comes in the history of each one of us, the event becomes a simple transition.

The writer of Revelation has stated it well: "Blessed are those who do His commandments that they may have the right to the tree of life, and may enter through the gated into the city" (Rev. 22:14).

In one sense our celebration of Bernadine's life comes from all of these measures. There has been an accumulation of years. There have been many personal accomplishments. The historical circumstances in which her life was lived were momentous. But the most important measure is recorded in terms of preparation. She took seriously this mortal life, and she never forgot the life that will endure the storms of time and the fires of judgment. Her preparation for life was complete.

Both the psalmist and the writer of Revelation described the mortal life of Bernadine Robinson, our departed friend. Yes, her days were threescore and ten, plus; but, more importantly, she has kept the commandments. She has been given the right to the tree of life and now has entered through the gates of the city. That event is worthy of our celebration.

Bernadine was a lover of books – I would like to conclude this eulogy with the words of a poem that epitomized this beautiful, wonderful lady.

I AM LIVING NOW TO LIVE AGAIN

I am living now to live again,
for life is too good to close;
as the body breaks with the weight of years,
the soul the stronger grows.

I am living now to live again,
for God within leads on
from dream to deed, from deed to dream,
and shall when earth is gone.

I am living now to live again
as spirit values will;
for the soul I build of spirit stuff
no death can ever kill.

I am living now to live again,
if a God of love there be;
for my love in His love cannot die
in all eternity.

I am living now to live again –
flesh and bone will turn to dust;
but my soul, a part of the eternal God,
can live, will live, it must.

That poem by Chauncey R. Piety described the life that Bernadine Robinson lived.

Let us pray:

God, give us grace to consider the way our lives are being measured. May the life of this our treasured friend remind us never to ignore the quality of life at the expense of quantity. We ask our prayer in the name of our Perfect Example.
Amen

The Lord Gives and the Lord Takes ~ Jettie Nealy

August 2, 1995

We are gathered here today to celebrate the life of a truly loving, caring and unselfish woman – Jettie Nealy. The obituary recounts her experiences as a trailblazing pioneer at Parkland Hospital; productive years as a teacher and shaper of the lives of young people; and the years as a public school administrator. We are here to celebrate the wonderful life that she lived. We are here to offer comfort and support to the bereaving family. We are here to lift up the hope that we all have ~ death notwithstanding.

History is not cyclical, but linear. Life is an unfolding saga that is moving into the future under the all-powerful eyes of God. Our text refers to a man who knew well all aspects of life. He also knew that there was a rhythm to life that included good and bad, joy and laughter, life and death.

In swift succession Job had lost his property and his children. Yet in the midst of his great personal loss, Job was able to rely on his faith in God and say, "The Lord gave, and the Lord has taken away; blessed be the name of the Lord" (Job 1:21). There is a divine rhythm of give and take to life. The Lord gives, and the Lord takes away. In this setting for today, we would agree that all life is a gift of God. Our daily existence is a reminder of the gracious gifts of our loving God. Our own life as well as life all about us is not the evolvement of matter or a result of some cosmic accident. We are persons created in the image of God. We have a purpose and design from the Uncreated One. Job said, "The Lord gave". What does He give? Obviously, this physical life we enjoy and yearn to maintain is a gift of God.

God also adds quality to this physical life. Happiness is a gift from God. Even now you recall many hours of happiness with Jetty. Happiness does add a quality to life. Happiness makes everything better. God gave us happiness that we might be better people. Memories of happy events in the life of Jetty will continue to warm the hearts of the family, as well as motivate them and us.

In this memorial service, there is another gift of God which we should not overlook. Saint Paul said, "Thanks be unto God for this unspeakable gift" (2 Cor. 9:15). That unspeakable gift is the salvation made possible through Christ Jesus. God's gift of salvation through His Son as the Savior of the world is what makes life worthwhile. It is that which gives us such joy. The gift of salvation allows our setting today to become a type of celebration. Salvation is God's gift to dry your tears, to lift the burden of death from your hearts and to comfort all who mourn. Death would be an unbearable experience were it not for God's gift. There is hope because of God's gift.

But let us go back to Job. He also said, "The Lord has taken away". We have hardly listed all these gifts from God when we are reminded of this setting we are in today. God has taken away. There are many losses in life, but now comes the greatest loss. The Lord has taken a loved one, and death has invaded a family.

A loved one has been taken. If we truly believe that He created life, we must confess that He has the right to do with life as He so chooses. Through this life of dear sweet Jetty He has shared a precious gift, and now He has called that life home.

In the process of doing so, the appearance is that God has taken back His second gift – happiness. No one expects you to be happy when saying good-bye to someone who has been special as Jetty has. Because God has been with us in Christ, He knows the sorrow of losing a loved one.

It is easy to be trapped and misled into believing that there is no happiness in death. We are primarily aware of tears and troubled hearts. We may even wonder if God has forgotten us. Then we remember His third gift which He has never recalled and suddenly everything begins to look different. As we remember the gift of salvation, hope shines through the gloom. Even through God has called home a life and the tears are real, in Christ Jesus we have a salvation that is steadfast and sure. Overarching and under girding of our gathering here is the fact of salvation.

If we see through the eyes of our faith, we can join Job and say, "Blessed be the name of the Lord". While the appearance is that physical life and happiness have been taken back, salvation through Jesus Christ has not been recalled. The Lord gives, but He does not take all His gifts back.

We must remember that all of life is in the hands of God. Faith will overcome grief which flows from the rhythm of our days. Through strength from our faith we can say with Job, "The Lord gave, and the Lord has taken away".

Because we are human, we grieve here and now. May we show the confidence of our faith by our personal testimony as we say, "Blessed be the name of the Lord".

Let us pray:

Lord, you have given and now You have taken from us.
Even in our grief and pain, we continue to call You "Blessed".
For giving us the life of this dear soul and the gift of many
memories, we offer our thanks. Most of all, for the gift of eternal
life which is never taken away, we offer our thanks.
In Christ's name – Amen.

Do Not Lose Heart ~ Ella G. Pugh

August 25, 1995

Burying someone that we love is not a new experience for most of us. The pain of heart and emptiness of spirit have visited us before when we buried a relative, or friend, and we are reminded again that all life is fleeting.

This death is especially hard for us. It is hard because Sister Ella Pugh was so young in spirit. We forgot her age. She was so young in spirit that many of us were not ready for her departure.

So, I would take nothing away from the grief that we feel today. I would not say that everything is alright. It is not. We hurt. We know we will hurt for a long time, and our grief is a dark valley we have to trudge through before we feel the warmth of the sunshine again. God made us so that we can feel the pain of grief, and it only means that we loved the way we were meant to love. We pay the price of love and courageously go on loving because the ones we love are worth it. We have loved. Now we hurt.

I say to you, grieve, long and deeply. Do not run from it, do not treat your grief as if it were a stranger you can send away, or deny it because someone who doesn't know better thinks it makes your faith look weak. Grieve what is lost, honestly, lovingly, patiently, until the cup is emptied. There is no other way back to wholeness, but facing what life brings.

As you grieve, think of the many things that you said to Ella Pugh in various ways. We told her that we loved her; that she was a treasure of a sister to grow up with; all a child could want in a mother; a wife beyond compare; that even if our relationship was brief, with few words spoken, or if we had only known each other on the surface, we still loved her, and loved her deeply.

As you grieve, be reminded of the way that she touched us, down deep under our crusty exteriors. As you grieve, remember her smile that she blessed us with when we were around her. Remember that she showed us a way to live with goodness in the rocky places of life, and that we will miss her.

As we all grieve, think with me of a line that I found written in one of the books in my religious library that has special meaning on this occasion. There were words from the poet Tennyson that said: "Live pure, speak true, right wrong, follow the King – Else, wherefore born?" What a wonderful way to describe the life lived, and shown to us as a model, by Sister Ella Pugh.

Yet, as we grieve, I would speak a word of comfort. Christians don't need to fear death as pure evil. We know those fears well enough. I would point you now toward the promise of death, the pearl within the cold, hard exterior.

Paul said that we are not like those who have no hope, for we know death as the doorway to the Promised Land, a rest from our labors, a reunion time with those we have loved. More than that, it is the time when we see our Lord as he is, and we can only dream of such a wonderful thing. We can lay down the struggles of faith. Faith will have completed its work, we won't be assailed by doubts and questions any longer, and we will know the glories of God in ways we cannot even imagine.

Wouldn't it seem wrong if life were all for nothing; if all the struggle, the overcoming, the loving, the development of character and goodness and beauty and heroism here were all for nothing, if nothing so precious lasted but were obliterated forever? We know in our hearts that we shall live, that eternity has been placed in our spirits, and that in another world we will continue what we have begun here.

Paul tells us that our bodies of flesh and blood are perishable and we can let them go. Truly, dust to dust, ashes to ashes. But he finished triumphantly: "What is raised is imperishable...it is raised in glory...it is raised in power...it is raised a spiritual body."

Why should we doubt this? We have been changing all our lives! Who can recognize the adult from looking at the infant's picture? In the plant and animal world a small round acorn perishes in the ground and a towering oak tree is raised, an egg perishes and a little yellow chick is raised, a caterpillar is raised from its tomb in the cocoon as a beautiful butterfly, and so we may expect the same for our dearly beloved, Sister Ella Pugh.

We are like babies in the womb. An unborn baby has no idea what life outside the mother is like and could never describe a rainbow or love or a favorite pet. Nor can we describe the next life beyond the hints the Bible give us.

But we know that the life that Ella Pugh lived here has prepared her for the next phase, and we know that she shall be where God is, and we have nothing more we can ask. Thanks be to God for this inexpressible gift through Jesus Christ!

Ralph Waldo Emerson wrote, "It is the secret of the world that all things subsist and do not die, but only retire from sight and afterwards returns again." It's a beautiful sentiment but is it true? Certainly we know of one thing that retires from sight and then returns again: the human body. "We know..." said Paul, "that if our house of this tabernacle were dissolved we have a building of God, a house not made with hands."

Frohman said: "Why fear death? It is the most beautiful adventure of life." Whitman wrote, "Nothing can happen more beautiful than death." Scott's comment was "Death is not the last sleep but the first real awakening." James Drummond Burns said, "I have been dying for twenty years. Now I am going to live." Paul said it even better as we close, "Christ has brought life and immortality to light through the gospel." And in another place he wrote, "The last enemy that shall be destroyed is death."

Sleep on sweetheart – we will see you again.

A Service of Remembrance ~
Etta Ford Turner

October 2, 1995

Evening has now come for a lovely Christian woman – Etta Ford Turner. As we assemble here to celebrate her home going and to comfort her husband of nearly five decades, Brother Jesse Turner, we can be comforted by these words from the Gospel of Mark (4:35) – "On that day when evening had come, he said to them, 'Let us go across to the other side.'"

Life is like day. We have the early morning hours of babyhood. Then there is the morning of youth. Followed by the high noon of maturity. Then evening comes, and the day ends. That day has ended for Sister Ford, but we can be comforted in knowing also that life is measured in deeds.

Not just the passing of time. Not merely money-making and accumulation of material things. Not in fame or brilliance. Life is measured in deeds. We can marvel here today in the life of service that Sister Ford lived. Because of her giving and serving spirit and attitude, and outlook, and actions; we can say of her – happy is she who goes about doing good.

As evening comes we recall the activities of the day that has passed. We can see in clearer perspective the great moral principles of life.

Those things of real worth now stand out. The Christian grace takes on their true meaning. You who are here and were close to and friendly with Etta Turner can marvel at her genuineness, her life as a servant, the love that she and Jesse shared together.

Having taken a backward look, we can now look beyond the end. The end of the earthly highway gives me confidence in immortality. The end of the earthly highway causes us to understand more clearly that life is continuous, and that death is only a transition, a phase. The old moorings fade away as we dream of the heavenly home.

Our dear sister, has now moved to her place that has been prepared for. Jesus said in John 14:2, "I go to prepare a place for you."

The Master knows the heavenly home. He came from heaven to earth. While here he taught men how to prepare for life. He inspired them to look toward the heavenly home. We can grieve over her passing, yes. But we can take comfort in knowing that the Christian's life is to be at home with God. To live our best here, as Sister Turner did, is to be prepared to live over there. The heavenly home is a prepared place for those who are prepared to enjoy it.

Home is more than a place. Home is a fellowship of loved ones. Our heavenly home takes continuous effort to attain. Once attained, it means companionship with God. The Savior speaks to us in John 14:3b – "I will come again and will take you to myself."

Finally, I submit that Sister Turner has a special message for Jesse and all of her friends that can be captured in these poetic expressions. The first from an unknown author:

GOOD-BYE, TILL MORNING COMES

"Good-bye, till morning comes again,"
we part, if part we must, with pain,
but night is short and hope is sweet,
faith fills our hearts, and wings our feet;

And so we sing the old refrain,
"Good-bye, till morning comes again."
But could we know how short the night
that falls and hides them from our sight,
our hearts would sing the old refrain,
"Good-bye, till morning comes again."

Finally, these words from Catherine Nunley Wilson have special meaning, and utility, for Brother Turner. They come from Psalm 46:10 where the Psalmist writes – "Be still and know that I am God."

O, restless, troubled soul, BE STILL, and know that He is God, the
Lord.
That He will be your strength and say.
Then, all the winds which blow in raging tempest, over land
and sea, cannot upset the deep serenity that dwells within...
nor quench the constant flow pouring from God's white throne,
effulgently, when we ARE STILL...and learn His will to know.

BE STILL! And know that God will lead us on in paths we cannot
see;
that He will guide our faltering steps.
We shall not walk alone.
He will be near, whatever may be tide.
In the mad rush of life, it is His will that we should sometimes
listen, and BE STILL.

According to the eternal plan, the body returns to the earth as it was and the spirit to God who gave it. Of all that is material we say, "Earth to earth, ashes to ashes, dust to dust." But to the spirit we cry: Now thou art free. Free from pain and sickness and sorrow. Free from all the physical handicaps. Free to dream and sing and work and love. Free to greet old friends and new, and Jesus Christ and to adventure with them forever. Therefore, Sister Turner says to Jesse, and the family and friends –
"Good-bye, good-bye until tomorrow."

He was a Rock of Refuge ~ Raymond Douglas

October 14, 1995

The Psalms are so human. Reading them we can find ourselves saying, "I, too, have felt just that way!"

Yet these words are more than reflections of human suffering and despair. They are songs of praise and thanksgiving; they are melodies filled with yearning and desire. The Psalms are an honest reflection of faith, as something more than wishful thinking or childish belief. The Psalms take us directly to the heart of faith, by revealing the very heart of the human struggle with God. The psalmists make no effort to clothe human anguish with the thin garment of religious convictions. For the psalmists, faith is nothing less than trust in God's purpose and plan for each individual and for creation.

Not a blind trust and not resignation. Faith, as expressed by the Psalms, is not an attitude of simply accepting one's fate, whatever that might be. Nor is it that form of optimism which seeks to convince the self or others that ultimately, it will all work out alright. Faith is a sense of being connected with God in a way that allows one to be honest about hardships and limitations.

Faith is trusting that God will be God and that we can be human; faith acknowledges that we can't will God into existence and that no one can will God out of existence! Faith recognizes that human life is limited to a span of years while confessing that God is unlimited in the power to heal, restore, and renew our lives. Faith sees the presence of God in seemingly small and insignificant events: the smile of a child, the touch from a loved one, the word of encouragement from a friend. Faith is that powerful force in human life which will always have an effect on the lives of others.

Faith, then, is the one word that captures the essence of this person, whose memory we cherish. Raymond Douglas was no blind optimist. He was, however, a man of quiet faith. He held faith in his heart; faith in God and faith in his family and faith in his Christian community. Raymond was a builder and a mover. He knew that growth means change and that change can be difficult. Raymond had a deep joy in and respect for life. He had faith in each member of his family; he accepted each one, warts and all! Raymond had deep faith in the richness of the lives, and the potential, for the young people that he lived and worked with. His faith was expressed in loving care and devotion and in his desire to see each of you in his family, and all of those in his ever-expanded extend family, to see each of you become the best that you could be. He recognized his own shortcomings, and that honesty made it possible for Raymond to accept yours, and ours, as well.

I think that Raymond (or R.L. as those close addressed him) would not want us to speak of him in lofty terms, as though he were something more than each of us. And yet, I believe there was something very special about this man. I believe that first and foremost he was a genuine person; an individual with character and integrity. Yes, he had his personal struggles and difficulties, as we all do. But he lived that form of faith which is so very hard to find in our world today. He trusted God and loved his fellow human beings, and he never confused the two! Raymond's faith was rooted in God, and his love was always directed to others.

You will grieve, and your hearts will remain heavy for a time. That is as it should be. With time, I pray that the memory of this man, and his faith, will begin to touch you deep within. I pray that when it touches you, your inner eye of love will recognize how precious a gift he has given. And I hope that his gift to you will not be lost in silence and indifference. For the God who touched Raymond's life, who sustained him throughout his times of trial, who strengthened him when he was weak and lifted him when he was in despair, that faith is there for you and me. And I believe Raymond would desire us to see and embrace and find comfort in God's presence.

Personally, I will long treasure the memory of this fine man. I thank our God for his life and his love. I will remember Raymond as a saint, as one who, time and time again radiated with Christ-like love. I, like you, will cherish his memory. Because Raymond taught us all well, that if Christ will never withhold his love from us, then regardless of what life holds for us, we must never withhold His love from others!

(Psalms 71:1-3)

Keep Your Heart ~ Pearl Montgomery

October 26, 1995

The well-known devotional entitled Our Daily Bread contains two pages that seem to reflect the life that Pearl Montgomery lived in a very special way. One reads, "She pleases God best who trusts Christ most." And the other reads, "While the Christian must live in the world, she must not allow the world to live in her."

Pearl was a person of deep faith in Christ, our Lord. It wasn't the kind of faith that draws attention to the believer, rather, it was faith that always pointed away from the self to Christ. Her faith was like a quiet stream, running below the surface of her life, providing nurture and strength in times of trial and struggle. Her trust in Christ was evident throughout her life as she faced a variety of hardships. She always spoke of her faith with heartfelt conviction.

Pearl's faith was, like her character, soft and gentle. She expressed a deep and genuine concern for others. It wasn't so much that her heart was in her faith, as it was faith deep in her heart. This woman certainly lived in the world, with all its joys and sorrows. But I never felt that the world had taken a stranglehold on her heart. She held no bitterness or resentment. I was touched by this woman's sense of compassion and concern for others, and I was often inspired by her commitment to Christ and her witness to the power of faith.

She had a truly personal relationship with our Lord. I had the impression that Pearl talked with Christ, as one would talk with a friend. Maybe that's why this chorus was one of her favorites: "He walks with me, and he talks with me, and he tells me I am his own. And the words we share as we tarry there, no other has ever known." Simple words, revealing a profound faith!

But where I really feel the presence of Pearl's character is in the passage from Proverbs: "Keep your heart with all vigilance, for from it flow the springs of life." The heart is the center of all that a person will think, do, and say. The heart is the treasure chest, from which a person gives to others either "good" or "evil".

Pearl's heart, held open to friends and family, offered a treasure that was "good". She offered each one of you gathered here among family and friends, a precious treasure of love, loyalty and laughter. Her heart was filled with the "good things" of Christ (and not of the world), and she shared those gifts freely and graciously.

We tend, too often, to measure the quality of a person's life by the great contributions he or she has made to society or culture. But here was a woman whose life touched so many others with love and compassion. No great accomplishment in the eyes of the world! But what an accomplished life in the eyes of God: "She pleases God best who trusts Christ most!"

From the very center of Pearl's heart, we each received some joy, some courage, some hope. She opened her heart, and the springs of life flowed freely to each one of us. That, I believe, is the true measure of this woman's greatness: Her willingness to share generously of herself, her faith, and her love.

I also believe that Pearl's practice of daily devotion was an effort to keep her heart filled with the blessings of Christ. Not so as to hoard them and keep them for herself; rather, in the desire to remain filled with the grace of Christ and then to pour out that grace into the lives of family and friends. Her home and her heart were always open, inviting others to enter and be nurtured in faith. What more could anyone desire from a single human life, than to live out the grace of God with and for others. And that is exactly what Pearl's life accomplished.

I will long remember her smile and her generosity in sharing love with me and others. I will long remember her faithfulness with the Usher Board of this church. The dutiful manner in which she clicked the counter to determine the attendance at the Sunday worship service, the midweek worship service, the various special events in the sanctuary or the Family Life Center. The way in which she trained and counseled others will also be remembered by me and you, as well. The way in which she sold newspapers was a perfect example of Christ-like servant hood. Whenever we would visit together, I would leave her, refreshed and renewed. I knew that somehow, purely by grace, I had been in the presence of a person who knew and loved Jesus Christ our Lord.

Pearl will be missed. But the gifts she shared with us will never depart from our hearts. In the days and weeks ahead, those treasures of love and joy will begin to nurture and sustain you through your sorrow. And, with time, that love she shared with you and the inspiration she has imparted to each one of you will become the source of comfort and hope. "Keep your heart with all vigilance, for from it flow the springs of life." Keep your heart.

When Sorrow Comes
A Service of Celebration ~ Brother Eddie Ray Benson

We are to always remember that our funeral services are not for the dead, but for the living. There is no word that we can say which can reach the ear of Brother Eddie Ray Benson. There is no music, however sweet, that can touch his heart. And, although we would pay a tribute to him through this home going celebration for his faithful Christian life, this service is primarily for those who are gathered here today out of love and respect for a good man.

The question is frequently raised - "Was he ready to go?" We can thank God that our friend and brother settled this matter when he was young and when he decided to repent of his sins and trust Jesus Christ as his personal Savior. And since that time he has served Christ well, always being true and faithful to the Lord, and to the highest and best things of life.

Brother Benson has suffered a long illness. We hear these words, "Blessed are the dead which die in the Lord, for they rest from their labors and their works do follow them." The word "blessed" here means "happy." Not all those who die are going to be happy, but those who die "in the Lord" will come to know the supreme happiness that only God can give. Then we read, "Precious in the sight of the Lord is the death of his saints."

According to the Bible, every child of God is a saint. And every movement of the Christian's life is precious in God's sight. Then surely, when His people come to die, it is precious in God's sight. John Wesley said it well on one occasion, "Our people die well."

Again we read, "He giveth His beloved sleep." Oh how we struggle and strain, we worry and fret about this life. We become tired and worn out. We suffer from illnesses that change our life completely. But then God puts us to sleep for a while, as in the case of Brother Benson, and we wake up in glory. Again we read, "Absent from the body, present with the Lord." This body is put away in the grave, but the real person, the spirit, the soul is not there. Eddie Ray has simply left his worn-out body down here and has gone out to be with the Lord. Isn't that wonderful? "Absent from the body, present with the Lord." Frankly, when our time comes, we should be like Eddie Ray, glad to get of this old sinful, sick, weary body when that day comes.

Paul said, "For me to live is Christ and to die is gain." Does a man gain anything when he dies? Doesn't he have to leave everything behind, his home, his loved ones, his friends. Yes, that is true, but I believe Eddie Ray can say that he lived for Christ, and like Paul he can say that he will gain more in death than he could ever gain in this life.

Eddie Ray has now gained freedom, *freedom from all the aches and pains and sorrows and sufferings and problems of this world.*

He has also gained fellowship, *a sweet fellowship never before enjoyed by us in this life. Fellowship with all the great men and women of the Bible. Fellowship with all the great people of all ages. Fellowship with all the loved ones whom we "have loved long since* and lost awhile." But best of all, fellowship with the Lord Jesus Christ, who made heaven possible for us.

Death is certain and there is only one way to prepare for death. That way is through faith in the Lord Jesus Christ. There is no other way of salvation. "He that believeth on the Son bath everlasting life; and he that believeth not the Son shall not see life; but the wrath of God abideth on him."

You can be comforted in remembering that you did your best for Eddie Ray. You gave him the best medical skill and nursing care that could be given anyone. Now you can just say with one of old, "The Lord gave and the Lord hath taken away; blessed be the Name of the Lord."

You can be comforted in remembering that you will see your loved one, Eddie Ray, again. David said that he could not bring his baby back to this earth, but that he could go to him. Heaven is a complete place and surely we shall see our loved ones again in a land where we shall know even as we are known.

Our heavenly Father does not play favorites. We know that He does not pay attention to some and not to others. We also know that every once in a while - and certainly not often enough - a human being comes along and touches our lives in a very special way, and a very good, way. Eddie Ray Benson was such a person.

You the family members, and others who were touched by him, will receive continuing benefits and blessings from having known him. We are grateful to God for the life and witness of this Christian disciple. We know that he trusted the Lord, loved the Lord, and obeyed the Lord. You can proclaim that he made you all want to become better persons than you are, the kind of persons we can become when the Spirit of the Lord is invited and welcome to dwell in our hearts and lives, the way Christ lived in Eddie Ray.

Christianity is not a story about "way back when," but an up-to-date call to live in the presence of the Lord, according to His Word. Eddie Ray did this faithfully.

Our thoughts as we conclude this home going celebration are where they are supposed to be - on you, Lord. You are the One who gives us hope, and light, and joy. You are the One who breaks our bondage to sin and death. You are the One who provides us with our eternal home - the house of many mansions - and who gives us the peace that is everlasting, beyond death, and that this world can neither give nor take away.

You are the One who turns our sorrow into celebration, our sadness into joy, our loss into confidence. And we thank you, and give you the praise, the honor, and the glory. Thanks be to God our Father, for giving us the victory, the life that is abundant and eternal; through Jesus Christ, our crucified, risen, and living Lord - now and forever.

So may God bless the memory of this good man, Eddie Ray Benson. And may He bless and comfort all of you who mourn today. And may all of us place our hands in the nail-pierced hand of Jesus and follow Him until He takes us home.

That Your Days may be Prolonged
The Home going Service ~
Brother Chleo James (Dent. 5:16)

How do you measure the quality of a person's life? How do you come to understand a person's life to have been meaningful; in particular as you stand on this side of death, and he has passed over that great divide? I believe we can see the meaningfulness and the quality of a person's life most clearly when the measuring device is the Word of God. We can take this great yardstick of God's and lay it across any person's life span, and it will reveal the richness or the barrenness, the fruitfulness or the fruitlessness of one's life.

The commandments of God form the particular order of the measure and quality of life. These words that have thundered over the centuries with the voice that boomed "You shall," "You shall not," and "Neither shall you" point us in the direction God would have us take. These words are not meant to frighten, rather they are given out of love and concern; they reveal the pathway that leads to life and health, to joy and fulfillment. These words oppose all devices we would use to measure the value of a person's life and call our methods of measurement into question.

You could never measure the quality of Chleo's life, as we so often choose to do, by the wealth and richness of his material possessions.

He had little in the way of worldly goods. And we could never adequately measure the quality of Chleo's life by his many friends and family members. He lived very much to himself, and his small family. We could not measure the quality of Chleo's life by considering the great contributions of talent and energy he left behind for all succeeding generations. He wrote no book, he passed along no great information, he made no contribution to science. These are the values we as humans use.

In the sight of God, Chleo's life was of great value and worth. Why? Because he followed the command of God, he listened to the voice that would insure a rich and full life. While we look to the great and glorious accomplishments of a person as the measure of his or her value, the Lord fixes his gaze upon the seemingly small and insignificant events, such as caring for and remaining faithful to one's parents and other family members. It is to be the person who follows this command that God promises "prolonged days" and that all "may go well."

The divine measure, laid across the life of this man, reveals the true quality of his being in the sight of God. His days were prolonged, and it went well with Chleo. The promises of God in this one command came to full fruit in Chleo's life, and that beyond all else makes his life both meaningful and of great value! Our measurement is temporal; God's is eternal. Our measurement is limited to the material and the practical; God's penetrates to the very depth of human existence, to the heart and soul. Our measurement ends with death, which is the very point at which God's measurement on the value of human life begins.

Chleo has earned his place at the table in the kingdom of God, not merely through obedience but through grace. We may deem his life small and insignificant, but then again the Word of God measures our value judgment, through these words of the Lord Jesus himself: "And behold, some who are last will be first, and some who are first will be last."

St. John Missionary Baptist Church
2600 S. Marsalis Dallas, Texas 75216

Resolution
on the
Homegoing Celebration
of
Brother Chleo A. James

It is with sad feeling that we record the passing of our brother in Christ, Brother **Chleo A. James**. He came into this fellowship April 21, 1991 from the New Hope Baptist church in Long Beach, CA where he served as a deacon and teacher in the Sunday School. Since being in St. John, he has worked diligently with the C. C. Harper Men's Bible Class and contributed regularly to the church until his health failed.

To the sorrowing family, Brother James has led a useful life in St. John. God saw his condition, so He eased his pains and gave him eternal rest. Remember,

Time is not measured by the years that you live
but by the deeds that you do and the joy that you give.
And each day as it comes brings a chance to each one
to love to the fullest, leaving nothing undone,
that would brighten the life or lighten the load
of some weary traveler lost on life's road.
So what does it matter how long we may live
if as long as we live we unselfishly give.

Whereas, Brother James' passing is a great loss to the St. John Missionary Baptist Church; we shall ever cherish his memory.

𝕽𝖊𝖘𝖔𝖑𝖛𝖊𝖉,   (1)   That we extend our heartfelt sympathy to the bereaved family.

(2)   That we, the members of the St. John Missionary Baptist Church, thank God for this life and for having had the pleasure to work with this great man.

(3)   That we strive to emulate his admirable traits.

(4)   That we bow in humble submission to the will of our Heavenly Father, and console ourselves by remembering that the sky remains parted and we can trace the passage and follow him within the gate.

𝕯𝖔𝖓𝖊 𝖇𝖞 𝖔𝖗𝖉𝖊𝖗 𝖔𝖋 𝖙𝖍𝖊 𝕾𝖙. 𝕵𝖔𝖍𝖓 𝕸𝖎𝖘𝖘𝖎𝖔𝖓𝖆𝖗𝖞 𝕭𝖆𝖕𝖙𝖎𝖘𝖙 𝕮𝖍𝖚𝖗𝖈𝖍 𝖔𝖋 𝕯𝖆𝖑𝖑𝖆𝖘, 𝕿𝖊𝖝𝖆𝖘, 𝖙𝖍𝖎𝖘 24𝖙𝖍 𝖉𝖆𝖞 𝖔𝖋 𝕺𝖈𝖙𝖔𝖇𝖊𝖗, 1995.

Dr. Wright L. Lassiter, Jr., Interim Pastor   Rubye M. Lipscomb, Church Clerk

The Short Step of Death
(The Time to go Home)

Text: 1 Samuel 20:1-4
Focus: 1 Samuel 20:3

The Homegoing Celebration for Ulysses S. Hammond, Jr.

To the family and friends, and this congregation, I commend your attention to these passages from the Gospel of Mark (Mark 13:32-37). "But of that day or that hour no one knows, not even the angels in heaven, not the Son, but only the Father. Take heed, watch; for you do not know when the time will come. It is like a man going on a journey, when he leaves home and puts his servants in charge, each with his work, and commands the doorkeeper to be on the watch. Watch therefore – for you do not know when the master of the house will come, in the evening, or at midnight, or at cock crow, or in the morning – lest he come suddenly and find you asleep. And what I say to you I say to all: Watch."

Throughout the time that I have known U. S. Hammond, Jr., I have been impressed by his strength, wisdom, propensity to serve, brilliant leadership qualities, and his noteworthy deliberate, but short steps. I now draw your attention to 1 Samuel 20:3 which contains a beautiful transaction between two dear friends: David and Jonathan. There was a covenant of friendship that embraced these two men as they determined a test to see what Saul would do next. David had been constantly running from an angry Saul. David was struggling to survive and maintain his life against the king who had set out to kill him. He had already escaped Saul's wrath on a number of occasions, but once again David found himself very close to this one who wanted to take his life. It was within this context that David made this statement, "But truly, as the Lord lives and as your soul lives, there is but a step between me and death" (1 Samuel 20:3).

It is also within this context of friendship and this covenant with Jonathan that David called upon his friend for help and companionship. And yet, one cannot overlook a certain amount of fear contained in the voice of David when he indicated, "There is but a step between me and death."

So much of our lives are spent in trying to stay ahead. We work and toil in our efforts to stay ahead of forces in life that seem to haunt us. Death is one of those forces of which we continually try to stay ahead. We think about it, we pray about it, and we consider it, both in regard to ourselves and our loved ones.

How many times do we pass close to that which could be death? As you travel on the highway, every time you pass a car you pass within inches of death. Sudden illness always bears the potential of death. No one is exempt from the fact that we are all only one breath away from death. For life is, indeed, very fragile.

David's statement reminds us all that for any of us there is a very short step-a very fine line-between life and death, at least death as we know it here on this earth.

Death is frequently something that we take for granted. There are times when we try to fool ourselves and, in our minds, push back the thought that death could ever be very close. We live and conduct ourselves as if our mortal lives would never end. But we need to recognize the truth. The truth is: there is but a short step between life and death.

Every life embraces experiences which serve to emphasize important facts. David was pursued by the jealous and envious Saul who hoped to push forward his kingdom by the destruction of David. David accepted this circumstance as a warning of the uncertainty of life and he communicated his deep feelings to his friend Jonathan. It is possible that this experience which calls us together today may have brought similar warnings to us, making David's statement very appropriate to our situation. For as David said, "But truly, as the Lord lives and as your soul lives, there is but a short step between me and death."

The very first thing that we must do is to recognize the fact that life on this earth is brief. David knew that his life lay along the borderline of death at any time. God's Word reminds us of the same fact: "They are as a sleep: in the morning they are like grass which growth up. In the morning it flourisheth, and growth up; in the evening it is cut down, and withereth" (Psalm 90:5-6). The tender grass blade, the budding tree, the blossoming flower, the shifting wind, and the ever-fleeing shadow – all preach to us of the gravity and even the uncertainty of life and the certainty of death.

The delicate nature of our physical bodies tells us the very same fact. Heartbeats are messages. Our breath which may at times be silent is but a reminder that life is a gift.

Our environment with all of its negative forces reminds us that life is a very fragile state. God's Word, our physical bodies, and our environment will not permit us to forget that there is, indeed, but a step between us and death.

Yet we must keep in mind that with all of these facts David did not allow the fear of death to freeze him. So it must be with our lives as well.

It is important that, as we consider death, we remember what death really is. What is that to which we approach so closely at times, yet touch only once? We can stand here today and claim promises based on God's Word that physical death does not mean annihilation. It does not mean total destruction. Death is not the end of existence.

Look at the world around us for a clue. Even nature teaches us lessons and reminds us that life goes on and on. What at first looks like the end of a cycle really is not the end of anything but the beginning of a whole new life. What looks like a dying tree and a dying plant is simply awaiting spring. What appears to be a withering flower is but awaiting a new bud. A seed will die in the earth, but a whole new plant will arise from its dying.

We do not gather here at these home going services for "Uncle U. S." to call attention to the end of his life. Instead we come here to claim a promise that what is happening before us is not the end of anything, but the beginning of an entirely new existence that comes through the belief in our Lord Jesus Christ. It is not an exit but, rather, an entrance.

Even though one short step separates us from this thing called death, when it actually occurs, as it has here, we discover that death is not what we thought. It is, indeed, so elusive! Death is not the destructive, totally mysterious force that we feared it to be. Instead, we will discover death to have been conquered already by our Lord who experienced it for Himself, and then came back to tell us that we should not fear death because He had made preparations for us. "Let not your heart be troubled" (John 14:1).

Flo Hammond would want me to say to all of you that we are here today to claim the promise made not only to her beloved U. S., who has passed from this life, but also to all who believe in the name of Jesus.

Even though, as David said, there may be only one step between life and death, once we experience that step we realize that it is not a giant step into the unknown. Rather, the step is a very small, short one into the arms of a loving Savior. Therefore, David's words come not as a threat but rather as a promise. That is why we are here, to celebrate the claiming of a promise made not only to U. S. Hammond, but to each one of us as well.

Let us pray:

God, grant us the grace to envision all of life as within Your love. Teach us to rest upon Your promise that preparation has been made for now and eternal life.
Amen.

St. John Missionary Baptist Church
2600 S. Marsalis Dallas, Texas 75216

Resolution
on the
Homegoing Celebration
of
Deacon Ulysses S. Hammond, Jr.

Whereas, It has pleased Almighty God to invade the ranks of the St. John Missionary Baptist Church, this time releasing from suffering our beloved member, Deacon U. S. Hammond, Jr.; and

Whereas, Deacon Hammond united with this church during the pastorate of Dr. Robert H. Wilson, Sr., he worked untiringly with the Deacon Board, Sunday School, Men's Fellowship, St. John Dallas Federal Credit Union, and the Counting, Budget & Control, and Building and Restoration Committees; and

Whereas, Deacon Hammond believed in younger men being led to do constructive religious work he trained Deacon Harry Green, Jr., and Dr. Gosby King for the offices of president and manager, respectively, of the St. John Dallas Federal Credit Union, and Deacon Stephen B. Hamilton for chairmanship of the Budget & Control Committee of the church. Deacon Hammond was a past president of the Downtown Kiwanis Club and was influential in recommending our own Deacon Gaylord Gray for membership in that organization; and

Whereas, Christianity and loyalty do not exempt one from suffering and death, they only assure triumph over death. The Apostle Paul suffered and died; Jesus Christ suffered and died for our salvation, and we too must suffer and die if we are to inherit what God has prepared for us from the foundation of the world.

Resolved, That we would like for his beloved wife, "Flow," and other members of the bereaved family to know,

Deacon Hammond will live in the hearts of the friends he made
And be known always for the foundation he laid,
Because Goodness and Fairness will never die
They go on shining like the sun in the sky.
Just as Honor and Truth endure forever,
Death is powerless to destroy or sever.
So his gallant soul has taken flight
Into a land where there is no night.

Done by order of the St. John Missionary Baptist Church of Dallas, Texas, this 1ˢᵗ day of November 1995.

_____   _____
Dr. Wright L. Lassiter, Jr., Interim Pastor   Rubye M. Lipscomb, Church Clerk

Celebrating the Life
of Sister Ethelyn Brown

"The Music of a Believing Heart"

A Tribute to the Life of
Mrs. Ethelyn Brown

Whenever a loved one crosses over to the other side, we who remain on this side are saddened over the departure, not the loss. But because we have faith in the power of God, we weep, but we know that when God calls us all home, we will be with our loved ones again.

Faith enables us to enter life's flow with some level of confidence. We need to have faith that if we open our eyes tomorrow – the sun will shine, air will be there to breath, and the earth will continue to spin on its axis! This is the kind of faith we all have to a greater or lesser degree. But this is not the kind of faith that gave birth to the beauty of the Psalms.

Only faith in God could have given birth to the Psalms. Because only faith in God empowers the heart to rise above the sob of sadness with a song of hope. Only faith in God enables the heart to sing, when sickness wraps its fingers around your life. And only faith in God can gift a voice with the courage to beat out a song of praise, when all others are silent in the face of a certain death and despair.

Faith in God enables us to see that life is so much more than the sum total of today's trials and tomorrow's headaches. Faith opens our eyes to the wonder of God as revealed in the glory of his creation.

I would dare say that faith gives voice to the music of the believing heart! So, while the rest of the world groans under the weight of discouragement, the voice of faith sings songs of hope in the promises of God. While other voices wail the mournful tune of death and decay, faith lifts up its voice with the triumphant cantata of resurrection and God's coming kingdom!

The Psalms sing from the heart of such faith. And the music of such faith is first born in the faithful life, the life that Sister Ethelyn Brown lived for almost eighty-six years. That is to say – long before the Psalms were written on paper, they were etched deep into the pages of life. The words were lived before they became lyrics! And the faith with which the Psalmist sings was practiced in the real world before it was penned on paper and set to music. That's why I have selected Psalms Ninety-two as a tribute to the memory of Sister Ethelyn Brown.

"The righteous shall flourish like a palm tree," wrote the Psalmist. "They shall bear fruit in old age, they shall stay fresh and green, proclaiming, The Lord...he is my Rock!"

Those words sound like the reflections of a senior saint like Sister Brown. Those words strike me as the words of a well-seasoned saint also. A saint weathered by time and trial and triumph. One who has known the pitfalls of temptation and the power of God's salvation.

To be sure, the words in our text sound human. They are the words of one sho has survived the fires of tragedy – on more than one occasion – whipping the dirt of an open grave from his hands;

someone who has fallen on hard times and lived to see his hopes renewed.

Someone, I would say, like Sister Brown. A person of faith and commitment and compassion deepened by the desire to serve God. Sister Brown served as a faithful member of the Sanctuary Choir for fifty years. Sister Brown was a soul absorbed in the will and ways of God.

But I want to call to your attention that there is a promise locked away in the words of our text in the Psalms. A promise that has been copied and rearranged in a thousand different hymns throughout the ages. A promise that will last beyond the shadows of time and into eternity. A promise embraced by Sister Brown, and now embracing her. The Psalmist writes: "The righteous will stay fresh and green."

That means that we shall live, long after age has turned our tired bones to dust – we shall live. And one day God will breathe his Spirit over the earth, and those who have fallen asleep in Christ will be raised to eternal life. That is the only promise that lends itself to a song of praise. And I believe Sister Brown would want us who have remained on this side for now, to learn the lyrics, and to sing that song with a resounding voice.

More important, I think that Sister Brown would encourage us to live lives harmonious with that hope. She would advocate that we live each day to the fullest – and to do so for the sake of Christ, and not our own gain.

I believe she would invite us to teach this song of faith to others who know neither the melody nor the lyrics. And above all else, I believe Sister Brown would admonish us to invite them to join with us in this choir of faith we call the Church.

I believe so because that's the kind of person she was. Mrs. Brown lived her life with the song of faith seeping through every pore of her being. Everything she touched turned to music that was bright and light, and beautiful. In fact, her life reflected a heart in harmony with God's love.

Which leads me to believe that Sister Brown's life was nothing less than music to God's ears. I imagine that whenever God turned his ear to Ethelyn, he heard a heart beating out the rhythm of righteousness and a soul wrapped in a song of praise to his name. I suppose you could say that Ethelyn Brown was a living Psalm! A note of praise here, a short lament there, but always the underlying song of thanksgiving.

But until that day, I believe that we who would honor the memory of this woman must be willing to receive and then live some portion of the faith she cherished. And to do that we must do as she did – commit to Christ's ministry of compassion. Perhaps we pay her memory no greater honor than to live our lives in such a way that we too can be certain that our hearts are in harmony with God's will – and our lives are music to God's ears!

Let us pray:

Lord, we entrust all our hours to You.
In our waking moments and in our sleep, we rest in You.
We also entrust this our loved one, Ethelyn Brown, to You in these moments of ultimate sleep.
Amen.

St. John Missionary Baptist Church
2600 S. Marsalis Dallas, Texas 75216

Resolution
on the
Homegoing Celebration
of
Sister Ethelyn E. Brown

She measured her lifetime in blessings, not in the years she has known.
Count up the number of people she touches, add up the love she has shown...
She measured her days in the gladness that she and her loved ones have shared.
Tally the smiles on the faces of friends, total the times she has cared.
Yes, she measured her lifetime in blessings, and she always remained in her prime
For youth is a feeling you keep in your heart whether you are seven or seventy-nine.

One writer has said, "One generation succeeds another, as wave follows wave," and so it is that though we mourn the passing of one who has proven herself faithful, loving, and kind, there remains another generation to succeed her, to follow the prints she has made upon the sands of time. A kind word, a helping hand, and a mind that led toward any who needed help. This was the life she lived.

Whereas, Deaconess Brown joined the St. John Church Family during the pastorate of the late Dr. Ernest C. Estell, Sr., she chose to help mold the lives of the youth by serving as a Sunday School teacher. She sang in the senior choir for more than fifty (50) years, and for almost fifteen (15) years she has worked with Deaconess Board "A".

𝖂𝖍𝖊𝖗𝖊𝖆𝖘, Deaconess Brown was a devoted wife and mother, one who always put the interest of her family first, who say to it that her son was given the best she could provide, in loving care, spiritual nourishment, and material comfort. The example she

𝕯𝖔𝖓𝖊 𝖇𝖞 𝖔𝖗𝖉𝖊𝖗 𝖔𝖋 𝖙𝖍𝖊 𝕾𝖙. 𝕵𝖔𝖍𝖓 𝕸𝖎𝖘𝖘𝖎𝖔𝖓𝖆𝖗𝖞 𝕭𝖆𝖕𝖙𝖎𝖘𝖙 𝕮𝖍𝖚𝖗𝖈𝖍 𝖔𝖋 𝕯𝖆𝖑𝖑𝖆𝖘, 𝕿𝖊𝖝𝖆𝖘, 𝖙𝖍𝖎𝖘 1𝖘𝖙 𝖉𝖆𝖞 𝖔𝖋 𝕹𝖔𝖛𝖊𝖒𝖇𝖊𝖗 1995.

_____   _____
Dr. Wright L. Lassiter, Jr., Interim Pastor   Rubye M. Lipscomb, Church Clerk

Keeping Memory Green

Celebrating the Life of Dr. Joe Watts, D.D.S.

"Moses took the bones of Joseph with him because Joseph
had made the sons of Israel swear an oath. He had said, 'God
will surely come to your aid, and then you must carry
my bones up from this place." (Exodus 13:19

In the passage just read for your hearing, I want to focus on a brief,
seemingly insignificant statement -- "And Moses took the bones of
Joseph with him . . ." That short statement is filled with profound
meaning, which has relevance for us today as we celebrate the life of
a friend, counselor, community servant, devoted husband and – in
short – simply a good man.

The children of Israel had lived under the whip and lash of the
Egyptian slave masters for a period of four hundred years. Then,
from among the Hebrews, God raised up Moses to lead them from
their bondage, organize them into a nation, and take them to the
freedom of the Promised Land.

After Moses attempted to negotiate their release with pharaoh,
aided by ten God-directed plagues, the time of their departure
finally came. Moses commanded the slaves to pack quickly and
secretly, and when the hour approached, to make haste to leave. The

Bible tells us that within hours nearly a million Israelites moved out of Egypt: "And Moses took the bones of Joseph with him. . ."

One may ask, why drag along the bones of a patriarch who had been dead for two centuries? Well, Joseph was that little Jewish boy who was sold by his jealous brothers in Palestine to Egyptian tradesmen who, in turn, took him to Memphis. With his ability and his talent, Joseph, upon maturity, became a statesman, the prime minister no less of Egypt. In this favored position, led by his faith in Almighty God, he brought his Jewish kinsmen to Egypt when a famine threatened their very existence,

Joseph excelled in faith, in moral practice, in wisdom. So they must take his bones with them on the forty-year journey, so they would not forget his righteousness, his leadership, his salvation, and his faith in, and dependence upon the one true God. "Moses took the bones of Joseph with him . . ." By this recall they know they were a keeper of destiny.

Today, we are figuratively carrying the bones of Dr. Joe Watts with us as a constant reminder of the kind of man and Christian leader and servant that he was.

> ➤ *We take the bones with us to remind us of responsibility and courage.*
> ➤ *We take the bones with us to remind us of righteousness and fairness.*
> ➤ *We take the bones with us to be reminded of his passion for love and forgiveness.*
> ➤ *We take his bones with us to remind us of compassion.*
> ➤ *We take his bones with us to remind us of unselfishness.*
> ➤ *We take his bones with us to remind us of integrity and brotherly kindness.*
> ➤ *We take his bones with us to remind us of patience and self-control.*

> *We take his bones with us to remind us of faith and loyalty to God.*

We are profoundly indebted to this man who was small in stature, but he was like a giant when it came to influence. He was like what radio stations call "the quiet storm." He spoke softly, but his words were so powerful!

He was also a very funny man in a unique way. I can recall his witty exchanges with deacons at the church. He was also pretty witty when he played golf. He could make you laugh. He never talked loud, but his words seemed to, at times, be almost like thunder.

So we take the bones of Dr. Joe Watts with us – "lest we forget; lest we forget."

A somewhat small in stature man, but he was like a mighty oak. So a mighty oak has fallen, for Joe Watts was like a tree planted by a stream of water, which bore fruit at the right time, whose leaves did not wither and dry up. Oh yes, he was truly a mighty oak!

And so we all feel a sense of profound loss. He worked throughout his life in service to others. He instructed us by precept and word to live self-controlled, upright and godly lives in this world. His roots were deep. He stood uncompromisingly in the storms and struggles here in Dallas.

In the last sermon that Dr. Martin Luther King, Jr. preached at the Ebenezer Baptist Church in Atlanta, he said, "if any of you are around when I have to meet my day, I don't want a long speech. I'd like somebody to mention that day that Martin Luther King, Jr. tried to give his life for others. I'd like somebody to say that Martin Luther King, Jr. tried to love somebody. I want you to say that day that I tried to be like them and to walk with them . . . I just want to leave a committed life behind. Then my living will not be in vain."

We remember Dr. Joe Watts as one who gave his life for others, who loved people, and as one who was a committed servant and leader. May the example of his life be emulated by us.

I say again, for emphasis, we are profoundly indebted to this great man. And so, we take his bones with us. Lest we forget.

Dr. Watts was a good story teller, so let me close this message with a story. Charles Dickens once wrote a story entitled "The Tale of a Chemist." The plot centers on a chemist who was terribly bothered about his past. A phantom offered to take away his memory, assuring him that it would save him from guilt and remorse, and thus become a great blessing.

So the chemist yielded to a shock treatment that completely wiped out his past. However, what was promised to be a great blessing was indeed a damaging curse. He no longer understood who he was. His life had no depth, because he had no sense of history. His life had no direction, because he was unaware of continuity. All of his life was "here and now," the immediacy.

His relationships had no meaning because they had no dimensions. The story closes with the chemist praying, "O Lord, keep my memory green."

As I go to my seat, I pray that God will keep our recall of the life of Dr. Joe Watts alive. Give us a sense of history that we might have an appreciation and know who we are, and where we are going. I pray that the Lord will keep our memory of Dr. Joe Watts green – and so, "Let us take the bones of Joseph with us."

Let us pray:

> *Dear God, who has inspired and led*
> *men in all ages to lead others,*
> *We thank you for the life of Dr. Joe Watts.*

We acknowledge his many honorable qualities.
We are grateful that he was a man of deep religious
convictions, who stood for the right and was always faithful.

We all feel a profound loss,
and we share the sorrow of his devoted wife Daisy.
Keep his influence ever expanding among us.
We commend his keeping to Thee, O Lord, confident
in the resurrection, through Jesus Christ. Amen.

Ready and Watching

Celebrating the Life of James Granville Lane

*"You also must be ready, for the Son of Man is coming
at an hour you do not expect." (Luke 12:40)*

*We come here at this time to share words of comfort with the
family of our departed brother – James Granville Lane. We begin
by offering to all who are here that at times like this; the Lord is still
very much in control. These words in the Gospel of Mark (13:32-
37) are particularly instructive at times like these. I offer them in
addition to the word from Luke that was first read.*

- *"But of that day or that hour no one knows, not even the
angels in heaven, nor the Son, but only the Father. Take
heed, watch; for you do not know when the time will come.
It is like a man going on a journey, when he leaves home
and puts his servants in charge, each with his work, and
commands the doorkeeper to be on the watch. Watch
therefore – for you do not know when the master of the house
will come, in the evening, or at midnight, or at cockcrow, or
in the morning – lest he should come suddenly and find you
asleep. And what I say to you I say to all: Watch."*

*Then we find in Revelation 14:13, equally instructive and helpful
guidance at times like these: "And I heard a voice from heaven saying,*

'write this: Blessed are the dead who die in the Lord henceforth.'
Blessed indeed, says the Spirit, 'that they may rest from their labors,
for their deeds follow them.' "

When I learned of the passing of this our departed brother through
his sister, Mrs. Janice Mason, I learned of a good family that arrived
here in Dallas and made a name for itself. It was a family where the
members loved one another, and also loved life. The family members
worked hard to be worthy of the gift of life that God provided to
each of them. A family that lived by certain important values that
are sorely needed today. A family where the act of reading was
treasured, encouraged and widely participated in by all.

This was a family populated with educators and persons committed to
education. A family where there was an interest in and commitment
to service to others; a family where there were some who believed
that life could be improved for many through business enterprise.

But most of all, this was a family where love was abundant
everywhere, and a belief in our Lord and Savior Jesus Christ was
shared by everyone.

In my talks with this loving sister, one gains a kind of picture that
causes me to now offer these words to the family as you celebrate
a life well-lived.

Every birth is the announcement of another death. Death is veiled
with mystery and draped in sadness. Keep these thoughts in mind
about death:

- Death comes to everyone. Every day, every hour, every
  moment death comes to someone.
- Death brings broken hearts, desolate homes, and vacant
  chairs. Childhood, youth, maturity are included.
- The time for death is not known. Our lives here are likened
  to that of a garden, where Jesus is the gardener. He may

pluck the most fragrant flower. You see, we are here but for a moment. And so, let us be ready and watching. Life is a challenge to live nobly. Life is a call to be prepared to live a long time, but ready to go at any time. So, as we live, so death will find us. Just be ready and watching.

As the sister of Brother Lane described how he indicated his desire to return to the hospital, it seems to me that he was ready and watching. This brings me to this final thought that we leave among these words of comfort for the family. The words are expressed in a poem titled Death.

<u>Death</u>

The word recedes; it disappears.
Heaven opens on my eyes, my ears;

Lend, lend your wings! I mount! I fly!

O grave, where is thy victory,
O death where is thy sting?

What is death? What is death?
'Tis slumber to the weary –
'Tis rest to the forlorn –
'Tis shelter to the dreary –
'Tis peace amid the storm –
'Tis the passage to that God
Who bids His children come,
When their weary course is trod,
Such is death!
Yes, such is death!

And now we say good bye. That thought is expressed in the words of another poem that is often read at times like these.

Good-Bye Till Morning Comes

Good-bye, till morning comes again.
We part; if part we must, with pain.

But night is short and hope is sweet,
Faith fills our hearts, and wings our feet;
And so we sing the old refrain,
Good-bye, till morning comes again.

Good-bye till morning comes again.
The thought of death brings weight of pain,

But could we know how short the night,
That falls and hides them from our sight.

Our hearts would sing the old refrain,
Good-bye, till morning comes again.

Let us pray: God, grant us the grace to envision all of life as within your love. Teach us to rest upon your promise that preparation has been made for now and eternal life. AMEN.

Because Christ Goes Before
– I'm Alright

Text: John 14:1-7 & 11 Corinthians 5:1

How could you and I find verses anywhere in the Bible more appropriate and meaningful for this moment than what we are sharing here today as we celebrate the life of a true warrior in the person of Senior Deacon George Gregory, Sr. By its own account, it is very difficult to say good-bye to someone special in our lives, but the invasion of death into our ranks forces us to do so.

One psychologist has said that two of the earliest words a child learns are hello and good-bye. And so we spend most of our days moving back and forth between these two words. As intense as the pain of loss can be under the best of circumstances, our grief would be unbearable if death was a great dark chasm into which our beloved Deacon Gregory were to fall and disappear.

The comforting words of Jesus form a stark contrast to our worst fears of death. His first six words in the passage from John set the stage for what He is trying to accomplish, and what God is saying to this family right now: "Let not your heart be troubled." Jesus is calming the minds of His followers made anxious by His comments in John 13:33: "Little children, yet a little while I am with you."

Jesus' word of advice and comfort to the disciples contained in our text is that they should exercise faith – faith in God and faith in Him. "You believe in God, believe also in Me." Our Lord also directs His words to those of us gathered in this setting -- "Let not your heart be troubled." We need to hear those soothing words today just as much as those anxious disciples long ago heard them. As Jesus observed His disciples, He saw them growing tired and weary. He is just as aware of the present circumstances of the Gregory family.

All of you have paid the price of exhaustion over the past few weeks during Deacon Gregory's period of intense hospitalization. To all of you who stayed with him around the clock, He says to you as well – "Let not your heart be troubled." These are not hollow words. They are a promise to each one of us.

If I may deviate from the text for a moment, let me share this thought with you. While visiting with the Gregory family in his last hospital stay, I noted a unique Father's Day card on a chest in the room. I opened it and noted the words printed, and the words seemed appropriate to share with all who have come to pay respects, and extend comfort to the family. The words describe Deacon Gregory most accurately.

> *You're someone the whole family feels proud of,*
> *Because deep within you we see,*
> *A person with character –*
> *Trustworthy and honest;*
> *And also as kind as can be.*
> *The values you live by make your very special,*
> *Inspiring us to be better too.*
> *You're someone the whole family feels proud of,*
> *And thinks of with love all year through,*
> *Happy Father's Day!*

Like those early disciples who were concerned about the imminent departure of Jesus, you too are touched because Deacon Gregory has gone on to be with the Lord. The disciples knew that Jesus was going away. Where, they did not know. In their hearts they must have known that death was involved somewhere along the way. This family has now confronted death directly.

Yet Christ told the disciples, as He tells you who are faced by all of these facts – do not worry. For their sakes He explained to them why they had no cause for great alarm. That message is for this family today.

First family members, you need not be troubled. That is a rallying cry needed in this anxious world that we inhabit. The image rendered in our text is that of an anxious mind. But Jesus says to you; don't let fear dictate your lives. Yes, we are always afraid that the worst will come. But Jesus Christ could say that even if it does, you still have no reason to fear. He verified His personal beliefs with His own life. Because He really did believe in God and did believe that God means what He says, Jesus was able to face the worst that life could offer.

You ask, why should we not be troubled? Jesus said, "Believe in God." This belief means never having to manage on your own. You can always go to Him and be helped by Him. We are to believe in Him as the One to whom we have already turned to many times and found to be true.

Second, death most certainly should not be our ultimate fear. Death is not falling into a deep chasm. Death for the believer translates into Heaven. The New Testament tells us that Heaven is a glorious place.

Jesus knows your anxiety at this point. You wonder -- "Did I do all that could for daddy?" Jesus tells us that every believer has his or her own personal and exclusive place in the Father's future plans. Deacon Gregory loved the Lord and believed His instructions. But

*as the end came, we are told that the last words to his nurse was –
"I'm alright."*

*Deacon Gregory is all right because he has so lived that preparations
have been made for him. Our coming and going in life is no accident.
Therefore, God has planned well this family.*

*Finally, the wonderful preparations have not been left to chance.
Christ has taken it upon Himself to make the arrangements for
us. We are important enough that the Son of God Himself has
taken care of our ultimate needs. When we encounter death, we
do not embark alone. Death does not take us by the hand. Instead,
Jesus takes our hand and leads us through a path He has already
traveled.*

*Friends, we would benefit ourselves by claiming our trust in God.
If we trust Him in this life, we can trust Him in the life to come.
There is no reason to be anxious or fearful. I tell you this because
Christ has gone before us and made all the necessary arrangements.
Indeed, Christ goes before us.*

*And so, calmly and quietly, we note the home going of this our
dear brother, who is known and loved deeply by so many. With
courage and determination we move away from this hour to accept
the responsibilities of those unlived days before us with the full
confidence that our loved one has only claimed the place prepared
for him by the Lord of life.*

*Let us pray: Our Father, we thank You that death is not the
swallowing up of ourselves, or our loved ones. We offer praise and
gratitude for the preparations made for each one of us. Help us
today to exercise our trust in You now and in the life to come.
AMEN.*

A Celebratory Prayer for a Saintly Man
~ Deacon Herman Parker

Sadness permeates this worship audience today. From the pulpit to the back door, everyone here has been touched by Deacon Herman Parker in a very special way. We all, myself included, have special memories of Deacon Parker.

Because we all serve a God of hope, I want to say to us all today that we have a right to grieve. Yet, Deacon Parker would say to each of us – look up. Hold your heads up high. Because God is good, and is a God of love, do not despair. Cry if you must, but do not weep too long. For I am now settling into my prepared place. I am moving into my room in the heavenly mansion.

We have come here to remember a man who accumulated many years. And yet his life can be measured in ways other than by the fact that his life spanned more than three score years and ten. His life combined numbers of years and accomplishments. His accomplishments never made the newspaper headlines. His many great acts of love were unnoticed by the masses. I must tell you that they were felt by those that he ministered to. Many of his labors of love were unnoticed by the masses. But, they were keenly felt by those that he ministered to. Many of his labors of love are known by only God – as they should.

Deacon Parker took seriously this mortal life, and he never forget the life that will endure the storms of time and the fires of judgment. His preparation for life was complete.

As Deacon Parker was a man of prayer, I want you to join me now as I life up a prayer of celebration for Deacon Herman Parker.

> *Our heavenly Father, we know that you do not play favorites. We know you do not pay attention to some people and ignore others. We also know that every once in a while, and certainly not often enough, a human being comes along and touches our lives in a very special and good way. Herman Parker was such a person.*

> *Not one of us here will ever forget him or fail to receive continuing benefits and blessings from having known him. We are all grateful to you for the life and witness of this Christian disciple.*

> *We know that he trusted, loved, and obeyed You. He made us all want to become better persons than we are, the kind of persons we can become when your Spirit is invited and welcomed to dwell in our hearts and lives.*

> *We know that Christianity is not a story about "way back when," but an up-to-date call to live in your presence according to your Word. Herman Parker did this faithfully, and we feel the summons to do the same.*

> *O Father, our thoughts at this service of worship are where they are supposed to be. They are on you Lord. You are the One who gives us hope, and light, and joy. You are the One who breaks our bondage to sin and death. You are the One who provides us with our eternal home – the house of many mansions -- and who gives us the peace that is everlasting, beyond death, and that this world can neither give nor take away.*

You are the One who turns our sorrows into celebration; our sadness into joy; our loss into confidence. And we thank You, and give You the praise, the honor, and the glory.

Thanks be to you, God our Father, for giving us the victory, the life that is abundant and eternal; through Jesus Christ, our crucified, risen, and loving Lord – now and forever. AMEN.

What Shall I Say of Her Life?

A Celebration of Life Service
For Wanda Roland

The preacher must always keep a tender and sympathetic heart. In that regard, funeral services must never become mechanical, or matter-of-fact. But some services come closer to the preacher than others. Such is the case on this occasion as we come to say farewell to this consecrated Christian woman. Her life meant so much to our church, to others, and to ourselves.

Let's talk first about my loyal and assistant who was always just plain Wanda. When you come to the end of the way, there is only one thing that counts. It matters not how much money you've made, or how high you have risen in the social circles. It does not matter how large a house you have lived in. It does not matter how many friends you had, or how many flowers cascade over and around your casket. The only thing that matters is your relationship with God through faith in the Lord Jesus Christ. If He is your Savior, all is well.

Now our dear and precious friend Wanda settled this matter long ago. She gave her heart and life to Christ, and she served Him well unto the end. She was never materially rich. She did not live in a mansion. She never rose to a high social position. But the true riches in Christ were possessed by her. At the end of the way, she inherited greater possessions than any woman or man in this world ever had.

What Shall Say of Her Life?

First, it was a life of helpfulness. Like the Master, she went about just doing for others. She touched many lives with her good deeds. She blessed many hearts because of her kind words. She lifted many people closer to God through her own consecrated Christian life.

Second, it was a life of humility. Although Wanda went out of her way and beyond the call of duty in being helpful, she never boasted about it. She always kept in the background, willing always that others would have the credit and that God should have the glory. Wanda would say with John the Baptist, "I must decrease, but Christ must increase."

Third, it was a life of faithfulness. Jesus said, "Be thou faithful unto death and I will give thee a crown of life." She was without question, a faithful saint and now she has gone out to receive her crown. The Lord and her Pastor, and her church, could always count on Wanda.

Fourth, it was a life that leaves a precious memory. During all the days that are left to her loved ones, they will be having many sweet memories of her. These memories will bless and enrich the family forever. As her loving treasures, you will remember the worthwhile things she said, and the unselfish things she did. Your lives will be the richer, and you will be drawn closer to God because of the precious memories of Wanda.

It was a life that tells of a blessed hope. When a Christian like Wanda leaves us, it is not forever. We have a hope; a hope backed up by the Word of God. It is the hope of another life, where we shall be with Jesus and where we shall see our beloved Wanda again.

We read in Scripture, "If in this life only, we have hope in Christ, we are all men most miserable." But we have this hope of a blessed and wonderful thing called eternal life. If this life is all there is, it isn't worth the candle. So we, today, thank God for a hope that is steadfast and true.

So on this day of celebrating the home going of Wanda, let us be thankful for a life well-lived. A life devoted to goodness. A life marked by faith in Christ. A life of unselfish service.

And let us be thankful for a God of all grace, who is with us in life, and in death, and throughout eternity. May God help us all to find our comfort and strength in Him, until at last we see Him and our loved ones face to face.

May the Keeper and Sustainer of lives be with us all. We love you Wanda Roland. AMEN.

Gathering at a Tender Hour

Celebrating the Life of
Sister Dessie Hart at Age 100

"But the path of the just is like the shining sun, that shines brighter unto the perfect day. The way of the wicked is like darkness; they do not know what makes them stumble."
(Proverbs 5:18-19)

There are many translations of this verse, but none is replete with imagery as the King James translation in our motto text read for your hearing. How appropriate that passage is for our gathering today.

Not one of us is here without bearing the influence of some special person in our lives. It has been said, and it is true, that no man is an island. That issue is not debatable. The only question is in what ways do we show forth this influence? If we are influenced daily by our contacts with people in general, how much more are we touched by those close to us?

Sister Hart. Mother Hart, Grandmother Hart. Mrs. Hart. "Lady." All of the foregoing represents words that we used to identify and describe this beautiful lady that we come to celebrate on this day.

We who are here should be grateful for the strong person that Sister Dessie Hart was. I would be so bold as to say that few people have the power of influence upon us as did Sister Dessie. She touched our lives in ways beyond our counting. Her influence at most times was quiet and subtle; but nevertheless it was clearly there. At other times her influence has been as bold and as obvious as thunder. She prayed with passion like thunder claps. Her light has been our path for decades, and that influence of this beautiful lady will continue uninterrupted even by her grave. For that small number of family members, she has shone light upon their paths since the moment of their first breath.

My friends, how much we owe this child of God who has cast light upon our paths. And how we need that light, for otherwise, darkness can be overwhelming. I recall the story of a hunter who was detached from his party and was stranded in the forest. However, he did not panic; he knew his friend would come for him.

In that story, it was a friend who came into the picture to offer guidance through a dark path. That is the way that Sister Dessie Hart was. She always stepped forward in a time of need and brought light to our paths. She was unlettered, but she earned the Doctorate of Loving Kindness many times over.

Throughout our lives we need someone to come to us and offer light on our path. So, my friends, we should thank God that Lady Dessie came this way and touched our lives in such a unique and loving way. For you see, Mother Hart brought light. Her influence was even more powerful because she brought the model of Jesus Christ in everything that she did.

Many of you have been touched by fervent prayers. Dessie Hart could pray the old-fashioned way. She was not an educated woman, but she could offer guidance and wisdom at the profound level. She was not a public speaker, but her sage advice made you stand in awe at the depth and pervasive quality of her expressions.

The Lord was so merciful to Sister Hart. When I would chat with her in her hospital bed, I would remind her that the Lord has put her in a better place in the hospital, for here she could gather her strength. She would immediately express thanks to God. Then she would say -- "Doctor Lassiter, I want you to know that God will remove every stumbling block. He has done that for me every step along the way. He will do the same for you, and I am praying that He will do the same for the St. John Baptist Church."

The Lord was merciful and kind in that she did not linger and suffer. She remembered almost every detail of the 100th birthday party that we celebrated with her at the church. She was so grateful and thankful for the many expressions of love conveyed to her. She also talked of making it to one hundred one. She almost made it there!

My friends, I believe that God, in His marvelous way, wanted this time to be a farewell birthday party for her. For like all journeys, this pilgrimage of Sister Dessie Hart came to end. Yet, she knew she was in God's keeping, and the end of the path was only a shadow. Such was her faith and comfort, and so is ours to be found.

Because of this fine lady, the heritage and legacy that she leaves for family and friends is a most valuable one. Family and friends, yours is the memory f a good Christian woman who was a "mother" to many, so you who remain can always remember, love and respect.

Her life has been light for our paths, and her death shall not conclude that influence. She waits for you; she waits for us and the pathway to her has been illuminated by her life and love.

So now we give her up and give her back to a Lord who has been her personal friend for over one hundred years. We who remain must take her gifts with us and not only embrace them, but incorporate them.

We leave here today much more aware that our lives are not islands unto themselves; That we bear the influence of special people in our lives. We will honor her best by leaving this place and going back to work for the Lord. But we leave realizing that to this date we have been blessed by the presence of a gentle spirit -- a beautiful Christian woman.

Let us pray: Oh God, we thank You for the light of Your Son and the way that light has shone through the live of Sister Dessie Hart. We thank you for her, and the life that she lived, and left for us an example to follow. AMEN.

He Fought a Good Fight – He Finished the Race

On Friday evening of last week, Deacon Lonnie Sanders lived out what we read in Mark 4:35: "On that day when evening had come, He said to them, let us go across to the other side." Evening came for Lonnie. The runner had crossed the finish line. The race was over. At evening time we can look back and reflect on these things.

- *Life is like day. There are the early morning hours of babyhood.*

- *Then there is the morning of youth, followed by the high noon of maturity.*

- *Then evening, and the day ends*

- *As we look back, we reflect on the fact that life is not measured in deeds. Not just the passing of time; not merely making money; nor fame or fortune or brilliance. But happy is he who goes about doing good. This we reflect on when we cross over at evening time.*

- *As evening comes we recall the activities of the day that has passed. As we see in clearer perspective the great moral principles of life. The things of real worth now stand out. The Christian graces take on their true meaning.*

For just a few minutes, Azalee and other family members, I want to talk about the race that Lonnie Sanders ran and won. I want to use the example of Paul writing to Timothy in 11 Timothy 4:6-8 as the focus of this short talk. As I reflect on Paul writing to Timothy, I can see Lonnie Sanders talking to young men here at the church.

Paul reminded Timothy that he was not a lone wayfarer, and that he lived in the sight of God who is both the observer and judge. Timothy was reminded that we are responsible to God for the stewardship of our lives. The way we use our days is of great interest to God.

Paul's age and circumstances add a moving tenderness to these words. This honest man of God had come to the close of his life and now looked back and used several images to convey his feelings. In verse 6 we read -- "My time has come." Death is not a great tragedy, but simply the home going of one who has a clear conscience and the report of faithful service. This is so true of Deacon Lonnie.

While Paul never used the word, he certainly implied the term victory as he gave an account of his days. Few verses in the Bible are quoted more often those this one in which Paul used the imagery of the games and made claim that he fought the good fight. He had not only participated in the game, but he had finished what he began, and he did it without losing the faith. When he appears before the judge, he will be crowned as the victor and given the wreath of a winner.

Paul describes his own life, not in boastful terms. He reminds us that all of life is a struggle. Further, the race is not over until the finish line has been crossed. There can be no letting up until the game is done. Paul suggests in bold terms that we must not only start well, but keep it up to the end. Indeed, keeping the faith becomes one of life's most difficult challenges. There are many rewards in life, but none compare to "the crown of a good life" (verse 8). Lonnie has his crown of a good life lived.

When Paul wrote these words to Timothy, he knew death could not be far away. Yet he was not afraid. He was confident of God in death as in life. For him it was but a normal way to conclude a life of service. As a result of these words, we may envision life from three perspectives, and I believe Lonnie would agree with me.

First, there is life which is in the past. Paul said, "I have fought," "finished," and "kept." Paul was saying that he gave the fight his best. He took life seriously and never took it for granted. He wasted very few minutes.

When a sense of joy one must have when one is able to look back on life and truly feel the best that you had has been offered to the Lord. Paul appreciated life and life is precious. Lonnie appreciated life.

Notice that Paul referred to the fight as a good fight. Why was it a good fight? Because his race was for God, and his faith kept him in the game. Paul said, "I have kept the faith." When our hour comes, will we be able to look back, as Lonnie did. Look back at the contest and ask, have you kept the faith? Paul did – and Lonnie did.

Second, Paul was referring to the life which now is. In his earthly state of mind, he was able to say "I am now ready to be offered." In other words, my work is done, and now is the time to move on; a move I am ready to make. Only a man of peace with himself and God could make this kind of statement. Lonnie was ready and at peace.

Third, Paul also pointed to the life to come. The apostle anticipated eternal life when he said, "Henceforth there is laid up for me a crown of righteousness" (verse 8). Most of us desire a crown, but do we really anticipate one? Christian hope requires both desire and *expectation. Think of the difference that kind of attitude makes in our lives now. Lonnie had that kind of attitude and expectation.*

There was no question in Paul's mind about his record. Death was not a tyrant, or a thief in the night. Death was but a way to claim the life which was to come.

In closing, we have gathered here to honor a good Christian man who has claimed the reward. The reward comes by way of a promise, and it is the same promise made to you and me. Lonnie Sanders has finished the race claimed the crown. Yet he would wish that we would remember that same crown is offered to all of who love the Lord.

Therefore Azalee and family, in the midst of your pain and grief, there can be a celebration. It is a celebration of life. Life that is past and present, but most of all, life that is yet to come. May we all run the race in such a way that we too can say, "I have fought a good fight, I have finished my course, I have kept the faith."

Let us pray: Lord, we realize that life is a race. As You observe and judge, give us strength to run the race with faith. Most of all, for those who have run before us, we offer our gratitude. Bless the memory of Lonnie Sanders as we follow his example toward the time when we too, shall cross over to the other side. AMEN.

PART TWO

Other Messages

Time, Talent, and Treasure

It is a special privilege to be asked to offer expressions at a memorial service for one that you consider a truly special friend, that you came to love as a colleague. When that special friend has touched the lives of so many people; when so many people have benefited from his wise counsel; when colleges and universities have advanced because of his sage advice; this is not a difficult task.

In the Gospel of Matthew there is a word in Chapter 25, verse 29 that encases the life of Bill Wenrich. It reads: "For to everyone who has more will be given, and he will have abundance, but from him who has not, even what he has will be taken away."

This text is described as "The Parable of the Talents." As a talent was a denomination of ancient money, it would appear that this is a story about money and its use. The master gave sums of money to three of his servants and the text tells us that the money was "entrusted," which means that the master expected to have it back. It was not a gift and not even a loan, for there is no reason to believe that the servants were in need; the money was given to the servants to be held until the master's return.

The text suggests that there was an expectation as to the use of the money, for it says that he gave the sums to each "according to his ability;" so not only were they not given equal sums, but their capacity to manage the sums given them was also unequal. Each did not start with either the same sum or with the same ability.

We know what they did with the money and how their ability was put to work, and when the master returned to settle his accounts, we know that the first servant had invested his five talents and got two more, thus giving seven back to his master.

The second servant had done likewise with his two with the same rate of return, and returned to his master four talents. Thus far the master has made four talents on the deal. The third servant, however fearing his master and being a cautious soul, did not risk his talent and returned exactly what he had been given, one talent; and we sympathize with this third prudent servant, for clearly he did not know his master. He thought that his master had more confidence in the others than in him and hence the small initial investment in his abilities, and he shared the master's lack of confidence in himself. Fearing to lose what little he had, "He went and dug in the ground and hid his master's money."

Now, if we were to rewrite this story according to our image of what a good master should do, we would have the master say to the now terrified servant, "There,, there, I understand your fear and your ambitions. I know you have a learning disability as far as figures are concerned and I know that you wanted to do what was right. It could be worse; you could have lost all the money in some foolish investment. As it is, you did the best that you could; I appreciate your concern for protecting my money. You can keep what you have. You could have made more, but at least you haven't lost out completely." This then would have a tale about the cautious servant and the forgiving master.

That, however, is not what the text says. The poor servant is harangued for his caution and deprived of the little money he has preserved by that caution, and the moral of the tale is that he who has will get more.

This story places a premium not on how to use and spend money but on how to use and spend time. Our loved one and dear friend Bill Wenrich used his time wisely and always to good end.

In his parables about time Jesus warns that what counts is not so much how we anticipate the future but how we use what time we have, what resources we are given, and how we redeem the present. The parable of the talents has nothing to do with investment and everything to do with engagement, of what we do with what we have where we are.

When the master in our parable went away he did not tell his servants how long he would he would be or when he would return. He left them with a splendid sense of insecurity, what the late Dean Samuel Howard Miller of Harvard Divinity School used to call "creative insecurity."

The text was to see how, living in that insecurity, which then as now was normal, one would manage, each according to his ability. The burden of the text is not "What do we do when he returns?" but rather "What is to be done in the meantime?"

The third man, the subject of the parable of the talents, suffers from what we may call a loss of nerve. He is given an opportunity and he finds himself in a state of paralysis. Filled with fear of God and himself, fearful that he will succeed, and fearful of the master, he plays the safest game possible; no risk, no fault.

Talent belongs to God; God gives us ability and opportunity that we might better do the work he has given into our hands, and in not using his talents to the fullest we cheat God by not giving full value. God requires that our ability and opportunity be put to use and that nearly always means put at risk. If a talent is to grow it must be put to use. The most gifted and profound talent, unpracticed, unemployed, never put at risk is as good as nothing.

The great Arthur Rubenstein was once asked why he practiced the piano so much. He replied, *"If I don't practice one day, I know it; if I don't practice two days, the critics know it; and if I don't practice three days, everybody knows it."*

A great talent or a modest talent, if it is to have the chance to do good things on behalf of the one who grants it, it must be practiced, used, and employed. If the talent is not used, if the gift is not practiced, it will be lost. As is said of privileges and athletic skill: *"Use it or lose it."* This is the saddest and hardest part of the terrible tale of the talents: The unimproved, unused talent is taken from the cautious servant, and the one who risked the most is given the most, and what remains for the cautious one when even caution is removed? Not very much.

This is not an example of taking food from the mouths of those who have to fill the mouths of those who have not. It is rather to say that those who dream no dreams shall have no vision; this poverty is not virtue; this poverty is the worst kind of impoverishment – the lack and fear of imagination. The cautious servant trusted neither himself nor his master, and in the end, like a criminal who is not allowed to profit from his ill-gotten gains, the servant is not allowed to profit from his lack of faith and action. He fails the course and is required to withdraw.

This is a story about time, about the right and good uses of time, and about the time in which we are found. It is a story as well about talent, not about money but about the ability and the opportunity that we have, in our time, to use it to his glory and the help of people here and everywhere. When we consider that our time and talent are the greatest gifts that we have, we understand them rightly to be our treasure, that precious cargo we are privileged to bear in this world.

This is also a parable about stewardship. You are asked in the time that you have to use wisely what you have been given.

This means that you must consider not only how you spend your time but how you spend your money, and how you use your talent as well. The gifts that you have do not belong to you; they are not yours to posssess but rather they are yours to improve, and if you do not, you will lose them. The parable, and life, are very clear.

We live in lean times; I know that you know that. There is a sense of urgency, even of despair, in the air, and we live under the threat of a cloud. Fear and caution abound, and you and I wonder what we can do. Life is harsh and unfair, and judgment swift and arbitrary. The rabbi tells us that when a wise man heard that the end of the world was near he went onto his garden and planted a tree, an act of courage, audacity, and hope – the only possible response.

If one were to have asked Bill to whom must we turn, when the winds of change blow over us, I believe he would say to all of us, what John Wesley said when asked what one could do for the kingdom, he replied:

> *Do all the good you can,*
> *By all the means you can,*
> *In all the ways you can,*
> *In all the places you can,*
> *At all the times you can,*
> *To all the people you can,*
> *As long as ever you can.*

So was the life of our friend, who was loved by his wife and children, and all who were touched by him. Bill used his time, talent and treasure wisely. Amen.

God is our Strength and our Resting Place

Scripture: Psalm 46 & Matthew 11:27-30

This is a time of celebration when we come together to bask in the warmth of a life well-lived by Dr. Angie Stokes Runnels. Let's talk first about Angie the person.

When one comes to the end of the way there is only one thing that counts. It doesn't matter how much wealth you have accumulated, or what your professional or social standing may be.

None of the other material accumulations matter. The only thing that matters is the relationship that you established and maintained with God, through faith in the Lord, Jesus Christ. If the connection was there -- all is well! Now our dear and precious friend Angie settled all of those matters a long time ago. That having been said, what shall I say of her life? Let me share three indelible defining points:

- *It was a life of helpfulness to others always.*
- *It was a life of faithfulness.*
- *It was a life that leaves a precious memory.*

An unknown sailor penned these words that capture the essence of her life.

God Has Been Good to Me

To tell in part demands new words.
His gracious power in so many ways,
Has blessed me through long years of happy days.
I have no eloquence to voice His praise,
I can but say with grateful heart,
God has been good to me.

God was good to Angie, and she was good to all who were touched by her. Now I believe that Angie would have something to say to her daughter and family. I found words from another source that somehow sound just like Angie. These words written by Chauncey R. Piety, have had meaning at memorial services for an extend period of time. Listen as I share them with you.

I am living now to live again,
For life is too good to close;
As the body breaks with the weight of years,
The soul the stronger grows.

I am living now to live again,
For God within leads on,
From dream to deed, from deed to dream,
And shall be when earth is gone.

I am living now to live again,
As spirit values will,
For the soul I build of spirit stuff,
No death can ever kill.

I am living now to live again,
If a God of love there be;
For my love in His love cannot die
To all eternity.

I am living now to live again,
Flesh and bones will turn to dust;
But my soul, a part of the eternal God,
Can live – will live – it must!

Now we must turn to words of comfort for Cynthia and the family members of Angie. One would be hard pressed to find stronger words of comfort than those found in Psalm 46. These words provide a sense of security for troubled times, even moments such as these today.

Psalm 46 is a powerful message of comfort. We have no way of knowing what caused the psalmist to pen these words. It is clear to me that some powerful force made him feel weak and afraid; just as this family is today. The psalmist was terrified over that which was happening to him. However, his faith allowed him to stand strong. That is my counsel to you family members also.

You see, there are times in our lives when we need strength and refuge when death intrudes in our lives. At those times there is no need to panic; no need for survival efforts; and certainly no need to give up. Only one act is needed in times like these: "Be still, and know that I am God."

Your burden today is deep and real. The burden of grief rests heavy with you. Yet we need to hear the words of Jesus at this point, and to heed His advice. For when He invites us to b ring to Him all of our burdens, the burden of grief is certainly included.

Finally, He tells you to bring Him your burden of grief and take upon yourselves His yoke. His yoke will be easy, and your burdens will become light. None of your burdens are excluded from this invitation.

What does that invitation have to do with grief? Everything! The burden you are experiencing now is one of pain. Jesus says to you *this very moment, bring that burden to Me, and place it before Me. When you do that, He will give you strength to bear what you thought you could not stand up under.*

When you take your burden of grief to the Lord, you are promised rest – beautiful rest. He will provide rest on the highest possible level.

As I bring this memorial message to a close, I want to remind you Cynthia and your family and friends, that Jesus is extending an invitation that you should accept. All that is required is for you to yoke yourself to Him in your grief. That simply means that you submit to Him.

Let us pray: Lord, help us to see death as it really is – nothing more than a shadow. Most of all, I pray, that You will help us to trust Jesus Christ who has experienced and understands all mysteries. O God, grant us that strength and courage to embrace our faith so that we may see that all of life is in your hands.

Deep within us we know the truth. You are the truth. May these painful moments never blind us to the reality of your certainty. Keep us so that we may abide in your shelter and in your presence. Give us the courage to take the yoke upon us and know that you will make our burdens light. Give us the courage to claim You as our fortress in times like these. AMEN.

Why Are We Here?

We are here today to celebrate the life of Dr. Frances Ford Hitt, Professor Emeritus of El Centro College. This is a massive assembly of friends of the Hitt family. We are all here to show our love and to be comforting to the family in this time of need. In my role as the President of El Centro College, I knew in a very special way this fast-moving, diminutive wisp of a teacher/scholar/servant. She represented one of God's choicest creations.

It would please me, and this family, if my colleagues from El Centro College, past and present, would please stand with me as these expressions is shared.

Our first reason for being here is to remember a fine Christian woman in the person of Dr. Frances Ford Hitt. It is good to remember, because our minds are gifts from God. Our memories warm us in moments of loneliness. Our memories also help us in moments of decision, which include grief.

Together, we claim the memory of Dr. Hitt's investment in our lives, and the lives of the many students that she interfaced with over the years of her service at this college. We should be reminded that memories of our loved ones are not taken with the passing of their mortal bodies. Through memory her influence will live on.

As we walk with people we are shaped by them. The good in one person can easily become the good in another. Some of you can honestly say that some of the good in your life is because of the influence and impact of Dr. Hitt.

Our memory is truly a gift from God, and can be the source of great joy as well. Certainly you will cherish the memory of this dear one. That is the way it should be.

There is a second reason why we have come to this memorial service today. We are here to offer comfort and support. The work of grief is never an easy task. Pain is part of our human experience; especially within the context of personal loss. Jesus understood that part of our humanity. He said – "Blessed are they that mourn, for they shall be comforted" (Matthew 5:4)

To the family, and especially David, the patriarch, through Christ our Lord, we offer support to you in this setting, and beyond it. One of the values of this incarnation is that God knows and understands. At this very moment He knows your pain and can help. Without the incarnation, there might be doubt in our minds that God really does understand our pain just now.

Therefore, we come together to offer support to a grieving family. That support is very important. Moving through this kind of experience without the aid of the Christian community must be difficult indeed.

Further, we come together to remember the life of a fine Christian woman and servant to humankind. We come together to individually, and collectively, offer support at a time of grief and sadness.

The words of the Apostle Paul are instructive in 1 Thessalonians 4:13: "Brothers, we do not want you to be ignorant about those who fall asleep, or to grieve like the rest of men, who have no hope."

Let hope embrace us as we move from this place. Let hope envelope us as we cherish the precious memories of Dr. Frances Ford Hitt.

May God's blessings be on each of you, and especially this family.

How do I Remember Louis?

It does not seem to be fifteen years since my family and I arrived at Bishop College, just across the street from this sanctuary on a late Sunday night. When we arrived at the Student Center, it was my surprise to be met by a delegation led by a cheery, bright-eyed young man who greeted me as "Mr. President." From that point forward, we developed a remarkable friendship and association.

How do I remember Louis? I remember his leadership with the Bishop College Minister's Lyceum. When he would take delegations of young preachers to pulpits in Dallas, other parts of Texas and across the nation. On those occasions pastors would welcome our young budding preaches to come and share with their congregation. Only the best of the young preachers would be selected for the reputation of Bishop College, and particularly the faculty in the Department of Religion, was at stake. Louis Kelly would always take great pains to give me a copy of the "report" from the visit. That is one of the ways in which I remember Louis.

I also remember the many sessions that the students had in the basement of the Carr P. Collins Chapel. My office was in that building and I would hear them down n the basement practicing their "whoops" before they even developed their messages; but that was all a part of the learning process.

Louis Kelly was a proud graduate of Bishop College and he went out into the world doing that which he had done so well in college – being of service and giving of himself.

After he left Dallas, we had little contact until I received a telephone call from New Orleans. The caller was the now "Dr. Louis Williams Kelly. He had prepared himself for service to our Lord and Savior. He was now working on the staff of Bishop Paul S. Morton, Sr., senior pastor of the Greater St. Stephen Full Gospel Baptist Church. Additionally he was the Dean of the Greater St. Stephens School and College of Ministry. I was overjoyed that we would be reunited again. Upon arriving in New Orleans for my assignment I marveled over the progress and growth that was so evident in this young man.

You all can testify that Louis was a learner. So let me tell you further what I remember about him. Every person in this world should be a continual learner. From the cradle to the grave, we are continually learning the great lessons of life.

We have some marvelous teachers – experience, sorrow, example, communion with God, and fellowship with the great people of the world. But on this occasion I want to tell you about a school that Louis was a star student in. A school where Christ is the teacher, Christ is the Master Teacher of al the ages.

It was said of the Master Teacher that "He spoke as One having authority." Louis sat at the feet of the Master Teacher during his life and I want to briefly recount the lessons that I know that Louis learned, and was mastering. Being a teacher himself, he would hope that others could learn as he did.

First, he came to know the Teacher. The most important thing about a school is its teacher, and Louis learned from the Master.

Second, he learned to pray. Third, he learned the spirit of Christ. Fourth, he learned of His suffering, death and power over the grave. Finally, he learned of his glorious home prepared for the redeemed.

Having learned all of these lessons from sitting at the feet of the Master Teacher, and being the excellent student that he was, Louis grew and prospered. Therefore we can now speak of the results of all the learning that Dr. Louis Kelly received.

First, Louis learned that he could walk with the Master Teacher in perfect trust. He learned that he was never alone. He learned that the Master would not permit anything to overcome over us. Not even death.

Finally, Dr. Kelly learned that he would become more consecrated. The highest gift to Him and to the world is the gift of self. Louis had a distinguishing mark as a Christian – he gave of himself unselfishly.

As a result of all the lessons learned, today is commencement day for Dr. Louis Kelly. No robe. No pomp and circumstances that we are accustomed to. But it is a glorious day in Paradise – for an honor graduate, Dr. Louis Kelly. He is standing before the Master to have conferred on him the ultimate in degrees -- the W.D. degree. What does it mean? It means simply "Well Done."

"Well done, my good and faithful servant. You have been faithful and loyal over a few things. Come on up higher and be of even greater service." The Master Teacher says: "You are graduating to service for all of eternity."

I pray that God's richest blessings will comfort and sustain the family.

Ready and Watching

A Memorial Service Message in Commemoration of Richard Lewis Hill

As I remember the moments that I shared with Richard during the time of our association from 1986 until the time that he went to be with the Lord, I was struck by his commitment to service. Of equal note was his deep concern for all of his brothers and sisters. Recognizing the deep concern that he had for his fellow man, I believe that he would want me to share a brief word of challenge to us from him. I believe that Richard would say – be ready and watching.

I believe that Richard would suggest that we pay careful attention to the Scripture contained in the Book of Ecclesiastes 3:1-8. "To everything there is a season, and a time to every purpose under the Heaven. A time to be born, and a time to die; a time to plant, and a time to pluck up that which is planted; a time to kill, and a time to heal; a time to break down, and a time to build up; a time to cast away stones, and a time to gather stones together; a time to embrace, and a time to refrain from embracing; a time to get, and a time to lose; a time to keep, and a time to cast away; a time to reap, and a time to sow; a time to keep silent, and a time to speak; a time to love, and a time to hate; a time of war and a time of peace."

Richard would also remind us of the wisdom of Luke 12:40 – "You must also be ready. For the Son of Man is coming at an hour you do not expect."

Every birth is the announcement of another death. Death is veiled with mystery and draped in sadness. Death comes to everyone. Every day, every hour, every moment death comes to someone. Death brings broken hearts, desolate homes, and vacant chairs.

The time for each of us is not known. But this we do know, Jesus is the gardener. He may pluck the most fragrant flower, as He did with Richard. But Richard would remind us that we are here but for a moment. Therefore, let us be ready and watching. That is the challenge for us to live nobly. That is a call to each of us to be prepared to live a long time, but also ready to go at any time. For as we live, so will death find us.

Because Richard not only loved life, he lived his life in the service of and for others. The words of a poem by Stephen Crane seem apropos on this occasion of our celebrating Richard's life of service.

In Heaven

In Heaven, some little blades of grass stood before God,
What did you do?
Then all save one of the little blades began eagerly to relate
The merits of their lives.

This one stayed a small way behind, ashamed.
Presently, God said, "And what did you do?"

The little blade answered, "Oh my Lord, memory is bitter to me,
For if I did good deeds, I know not one of them."

Then God, in all His splendor, arose from His throne,
"Oh, best little blade of grass!" He said.

Richard was that best little blade of grass. Constantly serving.
Always caring. Never selfish. Always giving.

We who constitute Richard's friends and associates must remember
that all of life is in the hands of God. Faith will overcome grief
which flows from the rhythm of our days. Through strength from
our faith we can say with Job -- "The Lord gives, and the Lord has
taken away."

Because we are human, we grieve here and now. May we show the
confidence of our faith by our personal testimony as we say, "Blessed
be the name of the Lord."

Let us pray: Lord, You have given, and now You have taken from
us. Even in our grief and pain, we continue to call you "Blessed." For
giving us the life of our dear Richard and the gift of many memories,
we offer our thanks. Most of all, for the gift of eternal life which is
never taken away, we offer our thanks. In Christ's name we pray
– AMEN.

PART THREE

End Notes

How to Give a Eulogy: The Lassiter Rules

I have been asked by young ministers to give them some pointers on how to give a so-called "good eulogy." The inexperienced then ask, "How can you summarize a person's life in a series of moments?" Know that it is hard – but I have learned to approach that special period after having labored over the opportunity. Note my use of the word "opportunity," rather than task, duty or assignment.

The first thing to know is that giving a eulogy is good for you. Remind yourself as you stand there, you are the lucky one because you were selected. Having been selected, you get to stand, face the assembly, the family, the world, and add up the life of the one being eulogized. You have been asked to do something at the very moment when nothing can be done. You get the last word in the attempt to define the outline of a life. To do this special service is a gift.

Let me quickly tell you that if on some level you are not interested in the problem of the assignment, this framing of a life, then you should simply decline the opportunity. Suggest someone else, if you can. Above all, be honest regarding the invitation that you have received and have chosen to decline.

Having accepted the invitation, you then must approach the task of writing and reading of the eulogy. Succinctly, the writing and reading of a eulogy is, above all, the simple and elegant search for small truths. They don't have to be truths that everyone agrees on, just ones that they will recognize. These are examples:

- *He protected his family above all else.*
- *She modeled notable women in the Bible.*
- *He was always on time.*
- *No task was too small, or hard, for her.*
- *He thought out every answer he ever gave before he spoke.*
- *She never wanted to talk about herself.*
- *He loved a good laugh.*

Always ask the family representative how much time has been allocated for the eulogy. They will probably tell you to take all the time you want. Time can be an insult at a funeral, therefore work within the finite space you have been given. Remember that the eulogy is just one part of the celebration.

As you stand there at the pulpit, consider the world as a series of concentric rings of loyalty. The people in the nearest ring, those in the front row, are owed the most. You should speak first to them. And then, in the next measure, to the room itself, which is the next ring, and only then to the physical world outside, the neighborhood, the town, the place, and then, just maybe, to the machinations of life-muffling institutions. Always remember the rings of loyalty.

It is a good practice to always write the eulogy. In grief, people ought not to be forced to wander through memories that may not be acute, well framed, and, above all, purposeful.

Depending on who is the departed one, the eulogist can be touched emotionally. Remember that a eulogy is not a chance to show off what you feel. This service is not about you. That is why you write it down. That is why you read it aloud until you feel in yourself every response you might have in every detail.

You must make the family, in particular, laugh during the service of celebration. Laughs are a pivot point in a funeral. They are your responsibility. The best laughs come by forcing people not to idealize the dead. In order to do this, you have to be willing (and able) to tell a story, at the closing of which you draw conclusions that no one expects.

In any good eulogy, there are moments of panic. Silences. Laughter in the wrong places. Moments when the speaker gets choked up. These moments – the tears or the silence – these are why you learn to pause and remember the concentric rings of loyalty. During a service, after a family member made a remark about something that I said, my response from the pulpit was (as I pointed my finger) "She knows what I'm talking about!" Everybody starting laughing. I could feel the family being touched in a special way.

My final word is always be prepared for the unexpected. These thoughts do not represent a prescribed format or plan for delivering a eulogy – just little nuggets from one who has been blessed and privileged to serve over seventy grieving families during my tenure as a minister.

Recommendations for Resolving Your Grief

- *Identify and feel all your emotions.*
- *Decide consciously to get through it.*
- *Accept support and ask for what you need – do not isolate yourself.*
- *Expect negative feelings and volatile reactions.*
- *Realize that your grief will be unique.*
- *Believe it makes no difference what others think.*
- *There is no one correct way to grieve.*
- *Remember that death will affect other family members also.*
- *Keep a realistic perspective about what you can expect from others.*
- *Do not think that you must fit your loss into your religious perspective right away.*
- *Do not let the needs of others determine your grief experience.*
- *Do not let well-meaning people minimize your feelings.*
- *Try to follow appropriate grief strategies that are offered to you by professionals.*
- *Remind yourself that pain will subside at some point.*
- *Identify, feel and express your feelings.*

- *Look for non-judgmental people who provide you with permission and acceptance.*
- *Realistically review and talk about your loved one and your relationship.*
- *Expect to talk about many of the same things repeatedly.*
- *Review all your lost hopes, dreams and expectations that went with your relationship.*
- *Identify and grieve for current and secondary losses that result from your loved one's death.*
- *Identify unfinished business and seek appropriate ways for closure.*
- *Yield to the painful grief process.*
- *Be patient with yourself and don't expect too much.*
- *Give yourself time alone.*
- *Cope with the practical problems you face as part of grief.*
- *Take breaks from grief.*
- *Find many new ways to replenish yourself.*
- *Don't make sudden important changes.*
- *Exercise and maintain good physical health.*
- *Take up an activity you always wanted to try or an old hobby.*
- *Take small risks.*
- *Have the proper perspective about grief; it will diminish, but you won't forget.*
- *Realize that a major loss will change you.*
- *Assimilate a new identity.*
- *Decide what roles to take on, which to give up, and which skills you must or want to learn.*
- *Form a healthy relationship with your deceased loved one.*
- *Decide on appropriate ways to keep your loved one's memory alive.*
- *Don't equate the length of your suffering to the amount of your love.*
- *Work to make the death of your loved one meaningful to you.*

The Wonders of Death

The Bible says many wonderful things about the death of a Christian. Our problem is that we don't believe these things. We think of death as an end to all things good. We think of death as a time of separation. We think of death as a hideous monster that has come to cut off all our joys.

But my Christian friends, and this family in particular, death for the Christian really is a wonderful thing. We should look upon death as rescue from a period of torment, torture, and trials. We should look upon death as a good friend come to relieve us. We live in a cruel world, a world of a few joys, but a world of many hardships, injustices, trials, tears, sorrows and separations. Now when death comes to take us into the presence of the Lord, where we shall have perfect health and perfect rest, wouldn't you say that death is, after all, a good friend? Let me encourage you to view death in that context. We look upon death as an enemy, but really it is one of God's servants who takes us to a better land.

So today we just come together to say good-by to our devoted family member and friend, and to thank God that he is now with Jesus, where sickness and sorrow can never touch him.

When the renown Dwight L. Moody lay dying, he said, "Earth is receding, heaven is come down, and I am going home." The same can be said of our departed friend. He has just gone over Jordan, he has just gone over to his eternal home.

A WONDERFUL TEXT

In Psalm 116:15 we read these words: "Precious in the sight of the Lord is the death of His saints." When a Christian dies it is a matter of concern to the Lord. He knows about every breath that we draw, every pain that we endure, every groan that we utter. It all means something to Him. Be reminded of what our text says. The text says that death is precious NOT in our sight, but in God's sight. The Psalmist is talking about death from God's standpoint.

Whether death comes suddenly or after a lingering illness, whether it comes in war or peace, whether one is killed accidentally on the highway or dies quietly in bed, it is because God permits it and I believe it is precious in God's sight.

So today the death of this our friend brings grief to family and friends, but it is precious in God's sight.

A WONDERFUL SLEEP

The Bible says, "He giveth His beloved sleep." This has to be the sweetest text in the Bible.

Now sleep is a very wonderful thing. We can't do without it. Every living thing must have some time for sleep. It "knits up the raveled sleeve of care." It brings us sweet rest and gives us new strength for the new day. Oh yes, physical sleep is a wonderful thing, but it can never compare with the sleep God gives to His beloved.

What a different sleep that is, indeed! We go to sleep tonight and when we wake up tomorrow, we have the same old problems and worries and aches and pains that were ours when we went to bed. But when we go to sleep in Jesus, we soon wake up on a new shore *and find that it is heaven. We breathe a new air and find that it is celestial air. We feel the touch of a new hand on ours and find that it is God's hand.*

THE MEANING OF DEATH FOR A CHRISTIAN

It means a change in environment: Everything down here has been contaminated by sin. On every hand we find dishonesty, drunkenness, lies and lust. And we also find all of the by-products of sin, namely sickness, sorrow, pain, poverty and death.

But when God's people die they go to a place where these things can never touch them. There is for them a complete change of environment. They go from sin to sinlessness, from earth's hovels to heaven's mansions, from earth's discords to heaven's harmonies, from all that is bad to all that is good, from all that hurts to all that brings happiness.

It means a change of nature: Here on earth we are burdened with an old carnal nature, which causes us continual grief. Up there the old sinful, fleshly nature will be gone forever. "This robe of flesh I'll drop and rise to seize the everlasting prize."

It means a reunion with our loved ones: You have stood by the bedside and watched your loved ones die. You have looked into their faces for the last time and wept many bitter tears. But they are not gone from you forever. You shall see them again in the land of light and love.

When our ship, the old ship of Zion, pulls into the docks of heaven our loved ones and our friends and our Savior will be there to greet us and welcome us to the Heavenly City. Isn't that wonderful? Isn't that reason for celebration and joy - today?

It means that we shall see Jesus: If it were not for Him there would be no heaven. The golden streets and the pearly gates and the mansions *and the robes and the crowns would mean absolutely nothing if Jesus were not there. But, thank God, we shall see Him and we shall know Him and we shall want to fall at His feet and thank Him for saving us and bringing us safely home.*

So now as we say "good-by" to this beloved family member and friend, we realize how wonderful it is up there for him. May his memory linger on in our hearts to bless us and bring us closer to God.

We live in a great and growing city. There are many cities like this in our land. But the city which has not been build with human hands is growing faster than all others. It is the Holy City of the New Jerusalem, which we call heaven. May God grant that we might so live and so trust Christ that someday we, too, shall join this friend in that wonderful city.

Our departed family member and friend is saying to us – I want you to join me. I want this to be your home too, and it can be if you belong to Jesus.

So, with Christ's peace in our hearts and Christ's hope in our souls, we say good-bye to this beloved one and we shall hope to meet him again one day at Jesus' feet, where the sunshine of His love forever shines and where we shall never grow old.

Prayer for those Living Alone...

I live alone, dear Lord, stay by my side
in all my daily needs, be Thou my guide.
Grant me good health, for that I pray
to carry on my work from day to day.
Keep pure my thoughts, my every deed,
let me be kind and unselfish in my neighbor's needs.
Spare me from fire, from flood, malicious tongues,
from thieves, from fear, and evil ones.
If sickness or an accident befall me,
then humbly, Lord, I pray, hear Thou my call.
And when I am feeling low or in despair,
lift up my heart and help me in my prayer.
I live alone, dear Lord, yet have no fear
because I feel Your presence ever near!

(Adapted from a book marker distributed by the Franciscan Mission Associates; P.O. Box 598, Mount Vernon, N.Y. 10551-0598)

My Body

My body is a bit of dust
In which the "I" of me resides
For the time of earthly tenantry;
When I cease to need it,
It will return to earth and be no more.

The "I" of me will return to God
Who gave me this bit of body
Through which to try my powers,
In it I have learned the lessons
Of weight, extent, direction and control;
And of suffering, sorrow, and self-denial.

These skills become part of me,
The sense of them can never leave me.
They are mine for all eternity.
They enable me to enjoy my house of dust,
And through it to glory with my Creator,
Here on earth as well as in Heaven.

Thus, I have loved my body,
As if it were eternal,
Knowing well that it is not so,
I do not wish to part with my body,
Though it is old and worn and weak,
But God has promised me a new body,
That will never grow tired, or sick, or old!

How wonderful! I think I will go see
What skills and lessons I can learn
Through the use of this new body.

You who know me here,
Will know me there when you come,
For that spiritual body will be "like"
My earthly "bit of dust," only it will be free of pain and death.

Borrowed – source unknown

Heaven – The Prepared Place

The Master knows the Heavenly Home,
He came from Heaven to earth,
He taught men how to prepare for life,
He inspired them to look toward the heavenly home.

He taught us about the Christian life,
The Christian life is to be at home with God.
Our souls are restless until they find rest in Him.
What is the heavenly home?
The heavenly home is a prepared place,
For those who are prepared to enjoy it.

What is this home?
Home is more than a place,
Home is a fellowship of loved ones,
That it takes continuous effort to attain;
What does the heavenly home mean?
It means companionship with Christ.

Borrowed – source unknown

Leave All to God

Leave all to God,
Forsaken one, and stay thy tears;
For the Highest knows thy pain;
Sees thy suffering and thy fears,
Thou shall not wait His help in vain;
Leave it all to God.

Be still and trust
For His strokes are strokes of love;
Thou must for thy profit bear;
He thy filial fear would move,
Trust thy Father's loving care,
Be still and true!

Know that God is near!
Though thou thinks't Him far away,
Though His mercy long hath slept,
He will come and not delay,
When His child enough hath wept,
For God is near!

O teach Him not,
When anyhow to hear thy prayers;
Never doth our God forget.

He the cross who longest bears,
Finds his sorrow's bounds re set;
Then teach him not!

If thou love Him,
Walking truly in His way,
Then no trouble, cross or death
E'er shall silence faith and praise;
All things serve thee here beneath,
If thou love God!

Borrowed – source unknown

The Death of A Precious Saint

Model Eulogy #1

Dearly beloved, we are assembled here today to pay our last respects to a devoted and precious saint of a woman. I draw your attention to our text from Psalms 116:15 -- "Precious in the sight of Jehovah is the death of his saints."

Let us pray: Our Father, and our God, we affirm that You are our refuge and our strength, a very present help in time of trouble. You are the eternal God and You are our dwelling place. You have promised to be near us when we call upon You in truth and You offer to us the assurance that beneath us are the everlasting arms.

We come to You, our Father, as a people who are hurting, feeling keenly the sting of death and the loss of a loved one. We would ask, that by the power of Jesus Christ, who Himself conquered the grave and death. You would be present with us and grant to us the comfort, the consolation, the grace, the love and peace which You alone can give and which alone is sufficient for us in this time of our need. May your spirit so be with us as we share in these moments of memorial that we shall fittingly remember our friend and sister, and give glory unto our Lord Jesus Christ, in whose name we pray. Amen.

*My brothers and sisters, members of the family of our sister who
has departed this life for an eternal life of sweetness and joy, we
pay our respects to one who gave her life to Christ as a girl, and
who has loved and served Him for well over a half century. Surely,
all the bells of heaven rang out when she left us and entered that
blessed city.*

*We thank God today for such people as our departed sister. They
live among us for a while; they bless our hearts; they make life
sweeter and better; then they gout to be with God and to await our
coming.*

We Can Judge Precious Saints by What They Love

*First, she loved the Lord. To her, the Lord was not some distant
person way off yonder in the blue. He was near to her. He was dear
to her. He was her daily companion. She walked and talked with
the King. She spoke often of her gratitude to Him for saving her and
for blessing her in so many ways.*

*Second, she loved her church. Because she loved Jesus, she loved
His church. Jesus put the church down here for us to live in and
serve through. If you love Christ, you are going to be faithful to His
church. And our sister was truly faithful.*

*She was a source of strength in the auxiliaries of the church. Nothing
except illness would ever keep her from attending her church. She
never shone in the social world, you never saw her name in the
society columns. But she gave her time and her talents through her
church, and she blessed more people by her Christian influence than
any number of society queens you could name.*

*Third, she loved her pastor. She always referred to him as "my pastor."
She loved her pastor because he was the Lord's representative.*

Fourth, she loved her Bible. It was always close to her. Her Bible was well-used and it was stained from use. Many a tear had fallen on its pages. Many passages were marked. The Bible was a lamp unto her feet and light on her pathway.

Fifth, she loved prayer. She believed in all the prayer promises of the Bible. She engaged in intercessory prayer for her friends.

Sixth, she loved her friends. Many of her beloved friends are present for this celebration service. She loved you and you knew it. I believe that many of you can remember her many acts of kindness that were all done out of a spirit of deep love.

Finally, she loved her family. Her family was the finest and best on this earth.

Some Concluding Words For the Family

Family members remember these four "R's" -- Rest, Reunion, Reward and Remembrance. A word about each.

Rest – She was tired and exhausted, but now God has given her rest. "There remaineth a rest to the people of God."

Reunion – Those who love God never part for the last time. In the vocabulary of God there is no such word as "good-bye." Because Jesus lives, we too shall live. And in that eternal life which never ends, we shall be reunited with those whom we have loved long since and lost a while.

Reward – God not only promises to take us to heaven, but to reward us at the end of the way if we have served well and for His glory. God will reward generously for those who have rendered faithful service here on earth.

Remembrance – You loved ones will never forget her. Her memory will always grow fresh and green in your heart. When you see her one day in heaven you will want to say: "I lived as you taught me and by the example you set."

Let me close this tribute to a precious and saintly lady with this story. A certain man's mother lived in his home and was a blessing to him and to his family. Each night as she climbed the steps to her room she would stop on the landing and say, "Good night, I'll see you in the morning." Then one night she passed away in her sleep. The entire family was broken-hearted, but they found comfort in remembering her last words – "Good night, I'll see you in the morning." They knew that when the night had passed away, they would see her in God's blessed morning-time.

So let this be your comfort family members and your Christian friends, she has just gone out to be with God, where sickness and sorrow can never touch her, and where someday you will see her again and be at home with her and her wonderful Savior.

So, with Christ's peace in our hearts and Christ's hope in our souls, we say good-bye to this beloved one and we shall hope to meet her again one day at the feet of Jesus, where the sunshine of His love forever shines and where we shall never grow old.

God bless you all.

The Wonders of Death

Model Eulogy #2

The Bible says many wonderful things about the death of a Christian. Our problem is that we don't believe these things. We think of death as an end to all things good. We think of death as a time of separation. We think of death as a hideous monster that has come to cut off all our joys.

But my Christian friends, and this family in particular, death for the Christian really is a wonderful thing. We should look upon death as rescue from a period of torment, torture, and trials. We should look upon death as a good friend that has come to relieve us. We live in a cruel world, a world of few joys, a world of many hardships, injustices, trials, tears, sorrows and separations. Now when death comes to take us into the presence of the Lord, where we shall have perfect health and perfect rest, would you not say that death is, after all, a good friend. Let me encourage you to view death in that context. We look upon death as an enemy, but really it is one of God's servants who takes us to a better land.

So today, we just come together to say good-bye to our devoted family member, friend and brother. We come together to thank God that our brother is now with Jesus, where sickness and sorrow can never touch him.

When the renown Dwight L. Moody lay dying, he said, "Earth is receding, heaven is coming down, and I am going home." The same can be said of our departed friend. He has gone just over Jordan; he has just gone over to his eternal home.

A Wonderful Text

In Psalm 116:15 we read these words: "Precious in the sight of the Lord is the death of his saints." When a Christian dies it is a matter of concern to the Lord. He knows about every breath that we draw; every pain that we endure and every groan that we utter. In all means something to Him.

Whether death comes suddenly or after a lingering illness; whether it comes in war or peace; whether one is killed accidentally on the highway; or does quietly in bed; it is because God permits it, therefore it is precious in the sight of God. So today, the death of this our friend brings grief to the family and friends, but it is precious in the sight of God.

A Wonderful Sleep

The Bible says, "He giveth His beloved sleep. Sleep is a wonderful thing. We cannot do without it. Every living thing must have some time for sleep. Sleep knits up the raveled sleeve of care. It brings us sweet rest and gives us new strength for the new day. Physical sleep is a wonderful thing, but it can never compare with the sleep God gives to His beloved.

What a different sleep that is. We go to sleep tonight and when we wake up tomorrow, we have the same old problems and worries and aches and pains that were ours when we went to bed. But when we go to sleep in Jesus, we soon wake up on a new shore and find that it is heaven. We breathed a new air and find that it is celestial air. We feel the touch of a new hand on our hands, and find it is the hand of God.

The Meaning of Death for a Christian

Death means a change of environment. Everything down here has been contaminated by sin. On every hand we find dishonesty, drunkenness, lies and lust. And we also find all of the by-products of sin; namely sickness, sorrow, pain, poverty and death.

But when the people of God die they go to a place where those things can never touch us again. It is a complete change of environment. We go from sin to being sin-free; from earth's hovels to heaven's mansions; from the discords of earth to the harmonies of Heaven; from all that is bad to all that is good; from all that hurts to all that brings happiness.

Death means a change of nature. Here on earth we are burdened with an old carnal nature, which causes us continual grief. Up there, the old sinful, fleshly nature will be gone forever. "This robe of flesh I'll drop and rise to seize the everlasting prize."

Death, as stated earlier, means a reunion with our loved ones. You have stood by the bedside and watched your loved ones die. You have looked into their faces for the last time and wept many bitter tears. But they are not gone from you forever. You shall see them again in the land of light and love.

When our ship, the old ship of Zion, pulls into the docks of heaven, our loved ones and our friends and our Savior will be there to greet us and welcome us to the Heavenly City.

Finally, death means that we shall see Jesus. If it were not for Jesus there would be no heaven. The golden streets and the pearly gates and the mansions and robes, and the crowns would mean absolutely nothing if Jesus were not there.

So now as we say temporary good-bye, we realize how wonderful it is up there for our loved one. May his memory linger on in our hearts to bless us and bring us closer to God.

We live in a great and growing city. There are many cities like this in our land. But the city which has not been built with human hands is growing faster than all others. It is the Holy City of the New Jerusalem, which we call heaven. May God grant that we might so live and so trust Christ that some day we shall join our brother and friend in that wonderful city.

Our departed family member and friend is saying to us -- I want you to join me. I want this to be your home also, and it can be your home if you belong to Jesus.

So, with Christ's peace in our hearts and the hope of Christ in our souls, we say good-bye to this beloved one, and we shall hope to meet him again one at the feet of Jesus; where the sunshine of His love forever shines and where we shall never grow old.

God bless you richly.

About the Author

DR. WRIGHT L. LASSITER, JR.

Wright L. Lassiter, Jr. was ordained as a Minister in the American Baptist Church by the Empire State Convention of New York in 1980. He was ordained for service in the ministry of Christian education.

When these messages were delivered he was serving as the Interim Pastor of the St. John Missionary Baptist Church in Dallas. Prior to the nearly three years of service as the Interim Pastor, he had served as an Associate Minister and Minister of Christian Education on the staff of the late Dr. Manuel L. Scott, Sr.

Prior to relocating from Upstate New York to Dallas in 1983, he served as the Associate Pastor and Minister of Christian Education for the Friendship Baptist Church in Schenectady, New York under the pastorate of the late Dr. Carl B. Taylor. He was licensed by his father, the late Rev. Dr. Wright L. Lassiter, Sr., who served as the Senior Pastor of the Mt. Carmel Baptist Church in Vicksburg, Mississippi for forty-six years.

He earned degrees from Alcorn State University, Indiana University and Auburn University. Prior to his ordination, he completed seminary training in Baltimore, Maryland earning the Doctor of Divinity degree. In addition to his academic and theological degrees he was awarded the honorary Doctor of Humanities degree by Dallas Baptist University. He has engaged in further studies at Oxford University in England.

While living in the State of New York, he served on the faculty of the Lay Academy of Schenectady, and was an instructor for the Congress of Christian Education for the Empire State Baptist Convention.

During his service at the St. John Church in Dallas, he served as a faculty member for the Northwest District Association of Christian Education, the Baptist Missionary and Education Convention of Texas' State Congress of Christian Education. He is a Certified Dean of the National Baptist Convention, U.S.A., Inc. He is frequently asked to assist churches in strengthening their programs of Christian Education. He also provides professional development programs for church leaders.

He performed supply pulpit duties on two occasions for the New Hope Baptist Church (Dallas) when they were seeking a new pastor. During the first supply service he conducted Deacon's Training and conducted the ordination for the entire Board of Deacons and coordinated the ordination of the Associate Minister, the Reverend Ronald Jones.

He serves on a large number of boards and commissions in Dallas covering the fields of education, religion, human services and business.

He is a professional speaker and a Distinguished Toastmaster and is widely acclaimed for his public speaking, professional presentations and sermons.

He is the author of ten books and numerous monographs and collections of speeches and sermons. He has preached, lectured, and taught in more than thirty states and internationally.

He has a long list of honors and recognitions that include two presidential appointments and four appointments by Governors of the State of Texas.

He is a life-long higher education administrator. He served as the president of Schenectady County Community College, Bishop College and El Centro College of the Dallas County Community College District. He previously served as the Vice President for Finance and Management of Morgan State University, and was Business Manager for Tuskegee University. Upon the conclusion of his twenty-year tenure as President of El Centro College, he was named the Chancellor of the Dallas County Community College District in 2006. In that role he serves as the chief executive officer of the largest community college system in the State of Texas that includes seven colleges, five community campuses and three administrative service divisions. The district enrolls 78,000 credit students and 25,000 continuing education students ranking it among the five largest community college systems in the nation.

He currently serves as an Associate Minister and Senior Pastor Advisor at the Concord Baptist Church of Dallas.

He and his wife have been married for fifty-two years and they have two adult children and two granddaughters. Their daughter is a bank executive with J.P. Morgan Chase Bank in Dallas, and their son is the chief executive officer of the Alameda County Hospital District in Oakland, California.

May 2011